THE CANON'S YEOMAN'S PROLOGUE AND TALE

THE CANON'S YEOMAN'S
PROLOGUE AND TALE

COMPANION VOLUMES

An Introduction to Chaucer, by M. Hussey, A. C. Spearing
and J. Winny

The General Prologue to the Canterbury Tales, ed. J. Winny

The Clerk's Prologue and Tale, ed. J. Winny

The Franklin's Prologue and Tale, ed. A. C. Spearing

The Knight's Tale, ed. A. C. Spearing

The Merchant's Prologue and Tale, ed. M. Hussey

The Miller's Prologue and Tale, ed. J. Winny

The Nun's Priest's Prologue and Tale, ed. M. Hussey

The Pardoner's Prologue and Tale, ed. A. C. Spearing

The Wife of Bath's Prologue and Tale, ed. J. Winny

Chaucer's World, compiled by M. Hussey

THE
CANON'S YEOMAN'S
PROLOGUE AND
TALE

FROM THE CANTERBURY TALES
BY

GEOFFREY CHAUCER

*Edited with Introduction, Notes
and Glossary by*

MAURICE HUSSEY

CAMBRIDGE
AT THE UNIVERSITY PRESS
1967

Published by the Syndics of the Cambridge University Press
Bentley House, 200 Euston Road, London NW1 2DB
American Branch: 32 East 57th Street, New York, N.Y.10022

© Cambridge University Press 1965

ISBN: 0 521 04623 8

First published 1965
Reprinted 1966 1967 1972

Printed in Great Britain
at the University Printing House, Cambridge
(Brooke Crutchley, University Printer)

For

I. B. *and* S. A.

CONTENTS

Acknowledgements	*page* viii
Introduction	I
Text	23
THE CANON'S YEOMAN'S PROLOGUE	25
THE CANON'S YEOMAN'S TALE	39
Notes	56
Appendix	74
Books for further reading	74
Glossary	75

The Brueghel engraving facing page I is reproduced by courtesy of the Kupferstichkabinett, Berlin

ACKNOWLEDGEMENTS

In the first place my thanks go to my colleagues, the other editors of the present series of Chaucer texts, and to our publishers for all their advice and encouragement.

Recent discussions of this text with classes have shown me the need for a number of alterations and expansions to the Notes. Annotation remains, as Dr Johnson saw, a 'necessary evil' but a way of showing the strength of the Tale that Chaucer left almost as an afterthought and critics have ungenerously dismissed. It is hoped that the existence of this edition has revealed this work to many who might never have found it in the complete Tales. The qualities of insight and poetic skill had in no way deserted Chaucer when he took up this subject: they are present to a marked degree.

Finally, it may be offered as some slight proof of the continued relevance of this Tale that in recent years I have encountered, both in person and in correspondence, a small number of both practical and esoteric alchemists. They see in nuclear science no refutation of their much older first principles. To them and to all who have sent me their comments upon a poem which came as an unfamiliar part of a great work I should like to express my appreciation and thanks.

M. P. H.

CAMBRIDGE

February 1967

The Alchemist: an engraving by P. Brueghel the Elder

to face page 1

INTRODUCTION

Even though Chaucer spent the last fourteen or fifteen years of his life, and of the fourteenth century, in composing and revising *The Canterbury Tales*, he was far from having completed the general plan when he died. Instead of recounting four tales by each narrator he had not even run round the company of pilgrims once, and he left such people as the Gildsmen and the Knight's Yeoman silent.

In most cases he was careful to assign a suitable tale to each narrator and to introduce him in a piece of verse-continuity (we know these as the 'link passages'). Yet since some of the links are missing, the complete order of the tales is in doubt. Certain blocks stand up as substantial units, such as the closing group which embraces the following tales: *The Second Nun's Tale*; *The Canon's Yeoman's Tale*; *The Manciple's Tale*; *The Parson's Tale*. These stories late in the sequence are not popular and familiar; but the *Canon's Yeoman's* is the most lively of the group. It follows close upon the *Second Nun's*, as the opening line tells. Where her tale told of the early days of Christianity, his throws a satirical light on the dark side of Christianity in the Middle Ages. It is, in addition, a piece of extremely full self-revelation by the narrator, smothered at times in regret and doubt but at others breathing the fresh air of optimism and longing for wealth.

With the Knight's Yeoman silent, we are glad to have a servant's idea of the world, and the Canon's Yeoman has a very special craft to represent, which was bound to prove interesting to every hearer and reader: the study of alchemy, which was partly a science and partly a magical practice.

The long narrative poem falls into two not very distinctly separated parts, a prologue and a tale. At the beginning, while the pilgrims are making their way through Kent and have recently paused at one of the stopping-places, an overheated rider pursues them. He is the yeoman or servant of a canon who is a part-time alchemist. First of all, he serves to introduce his master who is anxious to join them. When Harry Bailey, the host, questions the Yeoman in detail he discovers a man devoid of mystery and wealth, for he turns out to manifest only suspicion and poverty. The sales talk continues. It seems that the atmosphere of a pilgrimage induced people to lay bare their souls and reveal their confidences. The Canon, who fears exposure, hears it coming in his servant's tone of voice. He flees as quickly as he came and nobody cares.

Left alone, the speaker continues his prologue, with further self-revelations, and begins to explain the life of a laboratory steward of the fourteenth century and to show both the hopes and the despairs of his life as they shoot through his troubled and overheated mind. When this at last comes to an end, the tale begins. The central figure is a canon, though the Yeoman is at pains to say that it is not his master. There seem, later on, to be reasons for not accepting this denial, but they are not important. The Yeoman tells of a series of three different experiments with base metals and silver, and how in this way the Canon tricked a priest into thinking that mercury could actually produce silver under heat and pressure.

He had, of course, hidden a quantity of silver to be released at the correct moment and knew all the time that the genuine metal would appear at the end of his experiments. A lively narrative it is, but one that is also remarkable for the quality of the occasional reflexions upon the nature and purpose of alchemy, and an excellent example of self-revelation and rapid, colloquial couplet verse.

THE TALE

No matter how many of Chaucer's tales we know before we come upon *The Canon's Yeoman's Tale* for the first time, it must come as a slight surprise. One could almost assume that the poet expected readers to wonder why a new narrator had been sprung upon them, and to go on to wonder how many others might be necessary before the book was completed. Although it does not stand in the highest rank of tales, it has a considerable originality and as an attempt at explaining some of the actions of scientists of the period it is far too valuable to ignore.

Exactly why an alchemist was introduced we shall never know for certain, though it has often been assumed that Chaucer himself had been cheated by one and that he wanted an opportunity to release some of his own pent-up feelings. This may very well be, since a canon of Windsor named Schuchirch was known to have practised as an alchemist, although it cannot now be ascertained whether he was active during the period of Chaucer's stay in that town on official business. If we could accept the legend that Chaucer was tricked by the canon, it would explain some of the poet's financial difficulties at about this time and help us to understand at once why his alchemist had ecclesiastical status. In this case, the Yeoman's powerful complaints against his master become a dramatization of the poet's own emotions of shame and regret: they are emphasized enough in the poem to allow such an explanation.

Another explanation for the tale's existence may be that Chaucer required a rogue-tale again to maintain the balance of his long poem, and he had no suitable narrator who had not yet spoken left among the company. The topic of alchemy was popular in the thirteen-nineties, but in order to employ it in the sequence of tales a special narrator was necessary. This increase in his number of pilgrims allowed him to make the grand total of travellers 33, which is a finely symbolic number, consisting of two threes (three being the number of Trinity) and employing the number both of Christ's years on earth and of the cantos in the three sections of Dante's *Divina Commedia*.

F. N. Robinson, who is responsible for the most important modern edition of Chaucer's works, feels that there is no relation between *The Canon's Yeoman's Tale* and its predecessor, apart from the first lines that locate it in sequence in the most external manner. Yet with a further glance back at that predecessor, *The Second Nun's Tale*, we can question that judgement. The Second Nun told of the martyrdom of St Cecilia, known to us as the patron saint of music. Her steadfastness in the face of her tortures makes her an object worth our attention. When they attempted to roast her in a bath:

She sat all coold, and feelede no wo.

With this miraculous immunity she becomes a foil to the alchemists who sweat at their experiments throughout the

Yeoman's story. Later, she succumbs to the sword and triumphs over death in the manner of all martyrs. Here she succeeds spiritually where the alchemists fail: they have been sweating to change the nature of metallic dross to sovereign metal and to find the principle of life itself, but without success. Those who spend their lives in these experiments are shown to be in danger of losing their complexions from the heat, and Chaucer uses this image of physical discomfort to symbolize the deeper inner disorder and confusion from which they all suffer. (It must be noted that 'complexioun' has a much fuller meaning than the modern word; referring to a spiritual and moral beauty much more than skin-deep. Alchemists, in short, were endangering their souls.)

In the note to line 861 a further resemblance between the tales is discussed. But there is a quality about *The Canon's Yeoman's Tale* which is more outstanding and which subordinates it to the apparently inexhaustible *General Prologue*, the most succinct statement of so many of the poet's themes and ideas. In the lines about the Parson occurs this figure of speech:

If gold ruste, what shal iren do?

The proverb means that if the clergy fail in their own conduct they cannot maintain a moral leadership over their people. To give visual point to the case of the Prioress, Chaucer provided her with a gold brooch; in the case of the Monk it is a gold pin. Both ornaments were forbidden and symbolize their wearers' casual attitude towards ecclesiastical restrictions. The presence of so many ecclesiastical people in the alchemical workshops, searching for gold, makes the same point. Yet there is a cause for hope nevertheless. It was held by some researchers that the secret of making gold would only be revealed to those who were pure in soul. Bad as the two canons and the priest probably are, Chaucer wants the reader to keep an open mind and to review the problems of the uses of knowledge and riches with an alert judgement. In its own time, alchemy was not only a topic for burlesque. It was an exacting science with a carefully controlled order of activities and it ranged over problems of creation whose solution might at any time be revealed by God to man. It was, in fact, a type of creation with its own laws, principles and theology.

The finer aspects of the science are not elaborated by the narrator, who is presented as an ignorant man, unlikely to advance far in his profession—but it is through him that the story emerges. In his procedure we can discover the whole art of dramatic monologue which creates a narrator and tells a story at the same time. The Yeoman here is caught at a moment of momentous decision: he is going to abandon his master (he has good reason). In order to make up his own mind he makes his grievances explicit to himself and the reader is able to follow his reminiscences and understand his motives for action. He is a blower of the bellows and a sweeper of the floor and he rarely shows any greater understanding than these functions would give him. His manner of speech, the speed at which he goes ahead with his recollections and his narrative, is made perfectly plausible. He is inclined to repeat himself and ramble on, mixing warnings and regrets with lists of herbs and other experimental ingredients, alternating comic and pious remarks and reliving his life in a hurry. To make him stand up as a verbal creation, who exists only in the words given into his mouth by the poet, Chaucer retains the different styles of the lab. steward, the homespun philosopher and the science lecturer in one man who has been rushed on to the scene on horseback to fulfil an engagement. The changes of mood and the false starts are not necessarily signs of hasty composition: they are the natural expression of a disordered and disoriented man and they achieve the purpose of inviting the reader to ponder on the problems of the scientist.

The smaller matters of the laboratory come clearly out of the poem. The Brueghel engraving facing page 1 shows the keen-eyed investigator and his apparatus, and the miseries of this world come out of the poem extremely simply:

> lat swepe the floor as swithe,
> Plukke up youre hertes, and beeth glad and blithe. (383–4)

The duplication at the end and obvious jingle of the couplet catch the shallowness of the man and his baseless optimism about what he is doing. He has got nowhere in all his apprenticeship and his time is slipping away. The Wife of Bath looked back upon the past with her own vivid regrets:

> I have had my world as in my time.
> But age, allas, that al wole envenyme....

What the Yeoman has lost most obviously is his complexion; and this we are told on three occasions. What worries him more is that the outcome of so much labour is delusion:

> We faille of that which that we wolden have,
> And in oure madnesse everemoore we rave. (405–6)

7

That is all there seems to be in it for the best of them. The Yeoman is not as thoroughly grounded in the subtler implications of his craft as his master, so that he seems to be prattling into the void like the babbling Miller, Reeve and Pardoner or, above all, the Summoner whose Latin was of the same superficial order:

> Ay '*Questio quid juris*' wolde he crie.

This is the kind of man that narrates the tale. We may regret that he reveals nothing that is irrelevant to his theme. Brueghel's picture draws our attention to the penniless wife and children taken to the poorhouse as a comment on the lack of pence, while the experiments for gold proceed unabated. There is perhaps one aspect of the man that is not totally suppressed by the need to present the world of the laboratory. When he comes to describe the deluded victim Chaucer suddenly opens up a vein of romance, and imputes to the priest a range of emotions proper to the young lover in the tales of courtly love:

> Was nevere brid gladder again the day
> Ne nightingale, in the sesoun of May,
> Was nevere noon that luste bet to singe;
> Ne lady lustier in carolinge.... (789–92)

The Yeoman has lost the track of his story: many readers will remember the mood of the Squire in his efforts to 'stonden in his lady grace' when they read this incongruous outburst. It is correct for the Squire, but it is a kind of perversion of the emotion to sing of love in the pursuit of gold. The mood of the *General Prologue* returns; the tale that comes so late in the sequence is seen to be part of the working of the same purpose.

The Yeoman is made to break out into this passage, I believe, to show the world of romance as an escape from the mundane and familiar. Where the more learned men saw a world of romance in their speculations about the loves of chemical elements (a subject to which we shall return at the end of this Introduction) he was too earthy to understand, and he was left, as compensation, with the loves of squires and maidens, and the music of nightingales.

Chaucer rarely fits the teller to the tale with more completeness than he does here. What he is doing is to build up the man and his world at the same time, showing, as he does so, a knowledge of his scientific subject that no other poet of his time could rival. Nobody could ask more than this from even the most familiar of the *Canterbury Tales*.

There remain a number of problems. At the opening the Yeoman enters with his master who we may here call Canon I. In a few minutes the Canon flees as fast as he came. Incompetence as well as dishonesty seems to be imputed to him and he prefers not to brazen it out. Once he has gone the harangue develops. When at length the Yeoman embarks upon the tale proper we are assured that the charlatan who conducts the three experiments is not the same man at all, but another whom we may call Canon II.

An interpretation of this has been suggested in which the tale might even be a direct recounting of the Canon's last exploit before meeting the Pilgrims. Canon and Yeoman are both hurrying away to prevent discovery by the victim of the experiments and the confidence trick. They try, however, to give the impression that they wish to join the company and have hurried with only this in mind. It then emerges that the Yeoman is too indiscreet, and the Canon departs. Left alone, the Yeoman cannot resist blurting out the whole story, but realizes that he is revealing too much of his own dishonesty. He then finds that it is necessary to cover up his own part, invents 'Canon II' and asks with all innocence:

> This chanon was my lord, ye wolden weene?
> ...It was another chanoun, and nat hee.   (535, 537)

If he really is another man, why, we ask, does the narrator express himself with such animus against a complete stranger:

> the devel out of his skin
> Him terve, I pray to God, for his falshede,
> For he was evere fals in thoght and dede....(720–2)

To put it plainly, how does he know? The accent of truth is there, and one must assume that the two canons are indeed the same man and the Yeoman is either trying to shield his former master or else creating a situation in which all canons are one canon, all alchemists one alchemist, and all of them only human beings with problems of conscience. Poetically, the two people are to be identified and there seems no reason for continuing the pretence that they are distinct people.

Just at the turn of the fifteenth century, when the tale was written, there were special reasons for the serious discussion of this topic. Very soon afterwards, in 1403, alchemy became illegal in England, so discussion of it in the thirteen-nineties must already have had a sharper edge than we might suspect. Further, about seventy years previously, Pope John XXII had issued a papal decree against alchemy, so that when Chaucer was writing it was poised between a sin and a crime in public estimation.

To show a number of priests engaged in it was most meaningful to the instructed members of the writer's audience. One might exaggerate the position and say that the poem is a harbinger of official decree and the poet an unacknowledged legislator.

Crime or not, the subject is treated throughout the poem as a form of folly and blindness:

> Ye been as boold as is Bayard the blinde,
> That blondreth forth, and peril casteth noon.   (860–1)

Images of folly and blindness are found in other parts of the poem:

> O sely preest, o sely innocent,
> With coveitise anon thou shalt be blent.
> O gracelees, ful blind is thy conceite,   (523–5)

where it evokes the spiritual state of gracelessness and shows the sinfulness of the pursuit as well. At first, the canon's activities savour more of confidence-trickery than fully extended alchemy:

> To muchel folk we doon illusioun,
> And borwe gold, be it a pound or two,
> Or ten, or twelve, or manie sommes mo.   (120–2)

But the money is partially sunk back into the business and, we are made to feel, the investors are too gullible to be treated honestly:

> Lo, swich a lucre is in this lusty game.

From 'game' it becomes a matter of greater earnestness. Phrases like 'sliding science' and 'elvisshe craft' emerge, together with the name of Judas and other images of treachery to show us what the poet is doing. The complexity of the problem is conveyed in a passage which has, I believe, some of the complexity that we are accustomed to find in the couplet-verse of the eighteenth century:

> 'In the suburbes of a toun,' quod he,
> 'Lurkinge in hernes and in lanes blinde,
> Whereas thise robbours and thise theves by kinde
> Holden hir privee fereful residence,
> As they that dar nat shewen hir presence;
> So faren we, if I shal seye the sothe.' (104–9)

Superficially this is a description of the housing situation: alchemists are obliged to live in dingy areas. This in turn comes to define the nature of their work: it too is dark and dingy, the street and the art are both *blinde*. *Lurkinge* has all its modern connotations here and *hernes* are the dark corners in which the men are trapped. Trapped in the streets they are also prisoners of their delusions. *Fereful* conveys the fear of the outsiders and the different ones of the alchemists themselves. The great merit of this passage is that the poet had been forced towards complexity of language and rhythm in order to realize the situation. The science they are studying is one that 'slit' (slides) like the serpent and eludes human understanding. 'We faille of our desir', the Yeoman says and speaks for the whole race of them.

To add vitality to the verse, the vessels in the experiments seem to leap about the laboratory and up into the roof before smashing to pieces on the floor. The same speed is shown by the canon who fled 'for verray shame' and was gone. He is presented, however, as the typical alchemist in another more literal way. He is a rootless creature and something of an outcast in society; and this Chaucer supplies with his brief appearance. Traditionally, an alchemist was depicted as a man poorly clad; this is the man who might have paved the way to Canterbury with silver but has a completely threadbare overcoat. This precise image is to be found in many of the alchemists in literature and art, but it is Chaucer's particular genius to endow him with the images of haste, activity and the soaking bath of perspiration so that he is the human counterpart of some of the ingredients in his experiments. He is the extremely elusive spirit of alchemy which charges people with promises but denies them fulfilment, and does not stay to complete the course. More prosaically, he is the incarnation of the confidence-man and the defaulting debtor. In either of these roles he was liable to imprisonment and Chaucer probably intends the Canon to be interpreted in these ways as well as as an alchemist. All this we may see in his brief visit, though some commentators have made heavy weather of the reasons for his sudden departure. Nothing more seems to be required and this provides a further reason for accepting our solution to the problem of the two canons. There is only one and he is the personification of his profession.

The poet has other ways of expressing a distrust of the pretensions of alchemy. The list of substances used in the experiments shows Chaucer's familiar leaning towards the grotesque:

> Unslekked lim, chalk, and gleyre of an ey,
> Poudres diverse, asshes, donge, pisse and cley. (253–4)

Since excrement was commonly used in the maintenance of heat, no wonder then:

> For al the world they stinken as a goot;
> His savour is so rammissh and so hoot.... (333–4)

Our instincts are readily excited against such infectious contact and we cannot miss the association of the chemical brimstone with the 'fire and brimstone' of hell. Such symbols enliven the poem without disturbing the presentation of a fairly simple narrator's mind and style: it is the type of imagination he would necessarily possess.

At the very end of the poem, however, Chaucer was prepared to invade the work with a personal force and discuss the scholarly aspects of the alchemy which were familiar to very few people. At the end of *Troilus and Criseyde* he had already done much the same; he came from behind the scenes and produced a passage of moralization upon the disillusioned lovers and the falseness of pagan ideas. The notions were present in the poem but the epilogue made them more clear. Chaucer on this occasion drops the mask of the Yeoman and steps forward in order to bring the more thoughtful reader into the poem.

It is a late tale, and so it is not surprising that the movement and rhythm of the verse show particular mastery and that the handling of theme and image is equally subtle. Here, many of the couplets show a speech-rhythm rather than a conventional iambic metre and they are inclined to spread out over more than ten syllables. The writing, in fact, is much in the manner of late Shakespearian blank verse. It is impossible to call these three individual lines metrically perfect:

> We blondren evere and pouren in the fir.... (117)
>
> We mowen nat, although we hadden it sworn.... (128)
>
> And for a contenaunce in his hand he bar.... (711)

At one time scholars fought tooth and nail to discover ten syllables in every line because Dryden had thought the versification defective as a result of his ignorance of the sounded *e*. If two closely related lines are considered one after the other it will be seen that their accentuation is individual and not identical:

> By cause that I wolde yow atake.... (32)
>
> By cause that I am a lewed man.... (234)

Only a pedant would seek to accentuate them both alike: they take their sound from the travelling pace of thought. The following line gains its pace from the alliteration:

> He was of foom al flekked as a pie. (12)

From these examples it will appear—and the reader is free to find many more—that the process of reading Chaucer is as flexible an act as reading Shakespeare or Ben Jonson. The last line of the tale, far from being simply iambic, is composed of dactyls, spondees and a trochee:

> God sende every trewe man boote of his bale! (929)

And in the movement of it perhaps one can read the slight doubt in the voice: how many really true men are there to be rewarded? This is Chaucer at his most subtle, his narrator fully extended and at work: as in the similar creation of the Pardoner voice and the Wife-of-Bath voice, the most successful and highly individual speakers that the poet created.

The Yeoman voice often betrays a melancholy emptiness through his recourse to bare, outworn idioms:

> Al is in veyn, and parde, muchel moore.... (290)
>
> Right in youre sighte anon, without lie.... (574)
>
> Or somwhat elles, was nat worth a flye. (597)

It is a tired language as found in lines that droop limply over duplicated parts of speech: 'murthe and eek of jolitee', 'verray sorwe and shame', 'thise robbours and thise theves'. The dramatic tone is there but there is nothing underneath: the little man speaking is quite empty. A similar banality emerges from his excessive reliance upon proverbs: 'renne again a stone', 'rape and renne', and several others. Such devices diminish the speaker, whose pointless existence is heard between the words and the lines. Chaucer still has the mastery since he can command the boisterous and the jaunty on the one side and the alternating hollowness on the other: so doing he can re-enact the whole life of the mind. The speaker of all these lines is complete and he became the perfect mouthpiece for Chaucer's feelings upon confidence-trickery and alchemy.

In the ensuing centuries writers upon alchemy could do nothing but recommend the poem as the first time a great writer had ventured upon the topic. A most recent book on the topic, E. J. Holmyard's excellent Pelican, *Alchemy*, quotes the tale at length before passing on to consider the remaining works which stretch into the seventeenth century with the comic work of Ben Jonson.

Closely following Chaucer in the fifteenth century is the author of several minor alchemical pieces, George Ripley, a canon of Bridlington, famous for a long period for his work as an experimenter. Though his verse is of no high order it provides useful documentary confirmation of the techniques of the fourteen-seventies when he was writing:

> Som sought in Soote, Dung, Urine, some in Wine:
> In Blood, Eggs; Som till theyr thirst was gon:
> Deviding Elements, and breking many a pott,
> Multiplying the sherds, but yet they hit it not,
> Thence into Red Man, green Lion, Sol, Luna and Basilisk.

In this last line emerges the esoteric language from which Chaucer's tale is free and of which so much superb fun is made by Jonson.

The Bristol alchemist, Thomas Norton, a pupil of Ripley, also left behind a poem, *Ordinall of Alchimy*. This scientist claimed to have found the secret of the elixir, only to have it stolen from him by a lady. Further reference to this, as to all other English alchemical literature, will be found in Holmyard's volume. The line of alchemists continued with Thomas Charnock, Edward Kelly, John Dee and Simon Forman who all worked in the sixteenth century and provided the models for Ben Jonson.

Jonson was a writer capable of realizing the grotesque absurdities and finding the intense humour of their craft, since he had no belief at all in any serious purpose that could be served by it. His vivid comic imagination alone would have assured *The Alchemist* the place on the English stage which it has never lost: it presents the subject of *The Canon's Yeoman's Tale* up to date, in theatrical terms, strengthened by the same moral insight. *The Alchemist* is the one indispensable commentary on the topic that should be read by all readers of the present poem. In the notes there appear a few brief quotations from the play which offer the flavour of the dialogue. In the play as a whole once more a creative artist of the highest rank tackles the permanent moral problems in getting rich quickly as well as the incidental ones of exploiting a pseudo-science in the process. This is the final masterpiece of the tradition which stems from Chaucer's slighter narrative poem.

THE SOURCES

This tale presupposes two types of source. First, the original form of the fable of the cozening alchemist himself and his three experiments with one victim; secondly, the theory and practice of the science it documents. It has recently been discovered[1] that a highly likely source for a three-fold deception is to be found in the alchemy section in Ramón Llull's Catalan book, *Libre de les Maravelles del Mon* (*c.*1290). Three boxes containing gold and a melting operation in a cauldron occur in this narrative and Chaucer may have known of it in a French version. For the other variety, the field is extremely wide. The names of Arnaldus de Villanova and Senior are given in the text, and in the notes a little will be found about their writings. It is also known that Chaucer was deeply indebted to the first of the great medieval encyclopedias, *Speculum Naturale*, by Vincent de Beauvais who wrote over a century before him. In addition to information upon topics that Chaucer studied for use in other poems, Vincent provided a comprehensive account of the practice and terminology of alchemists, most of which is employed in this tale.

John Gower, a friend of Chaucer, and author of the long English poem *Confessio Amantis* (*c.* 1390), must also be singled out. He too was conversant with the sciences of his day and includes a fairly dull stretch of text-book verse in his poem:

> The science of himself is trewe
> Upon the form as it was founded

There are several pages of this but these are omitted from

[1] See *Notes and Queries*, January 1967.

the recent modern version by Terence Tiller (Penguin Books) and are extremely difficult to obtain. Where Gower looked for general principles and succinct statements, Chaucer sought out the fables and the human situations to illustrate them: Gower's contribution remains only for the specialist.

In the broadest sense, we return to alchemy as the most significant source of the poem. We have seen how it worked in the case of a pair of practitioners and must finally attempt to inspect the topic a little more broadly. It was commonly held that matter possessed a life of its own, a theory known as hylozoism. This gave rise to one or two popular ideas. It was thought that inside the base elements, such as iron and copper, there were the seeds of gold and silver, which could be encouraged to grow if the temperature and other conditions were carefully manipulated. Iron and copper were, in fact, anxious to grow into a better estate. Spontaneous combustion and generation were naturally expected to be the common properties of matter. Chaucer does not branch into a disquisition upon all this: he has his own means at his disposal. He writes concretely of the desire to find the gold inside the brimstone, of the metals that 'lepe into the roof' and the pot that 'was crased'. Thus he endows them with a life of their own and gives intense vitality to his poem.

The various experiments that were undertaken were seen as gates that opened the way for the new metals to be born. Powders and heating could provide the correct circumstances for the rebirth of the elements, and the alchemists were endlessly at work mixing, heating, cooling, dissolving and heating again to newer and higher temperatures. Special names were given to the different stages, not all of which are mentioned by the poet. From other writings of the period we derive these names of ten experiments, which were ten opportunities for error and ten steps to retrace again and again when error crept in. They are calcination, solution, separation, conjunction, putrefaction, congelation, cibation, sublimation, fermentation, exaltation, multiplication and projection. This is the technical description of what was being done in the laboratories, but Chaucer was primarily interested in the purely human activities. He reduces it to the bare essentials:

> Somme seyde it was long on the fir making;
> Somme seyde nay, it was on the blowing. (369–70)

Wherever it was, he says, the error entered into the calculations and in the long run

> He that semeth the wiseste, by Jhesus!
> Is moost fool, whan it cometh to the preef. (414–15)

It is a judgement that we find in several other tales where the interplay of the learned and the ignorant is the subject. As in *The Miller's Tale* or *The Reve's Tale*, Chaucer has reached the simplest of conclusions.

But the physical experiments were not the whole matter of alchemy: far from it. The Yeoman is, as we have seen, very limited in his understanding of the task and his superiors possessed a stock of secret lore that he either failed to understand or was completely unaware of. The medieval alchemist was seeking to be a creator in his own right. The great elixir of life, when it was discovered, would convey immortality and omnipotence. Such a pursuit became all-absorbing to some of the thinkers and so secret and clouded in metaphorical explanation that it is extremely difficult for us to be more clear about it than the Yeoman himself. The pursuit evolved its own vocabulary which was so esoteric in its reliance upon symbols that it is hardly profitable for us to persist with it today, especially since Chaucer's poem does not rely upon it. We may gain a hint of its nature if we realize that quicksilver and brimstone, two chemicals with known properties, were also, to the adept, something different. They were deities, the male and female forces in creation, that might produce new life and could only be understood in the language of poetry or symbolism. With this aspect of alchemy Chaucer seems to have had little patience, although at the end of the poem he recommends us to look at such authorities as Arnaldus or Senior where the ideas can be pursued. The Yeoman uses the word 'mistily' to describe this learning and one receives the impression that experts were not always in agreement and that most of the doors of such perceptions remained closed.

It is possible to explore the field of esoteric alchemy at the present day, because it has not died out. The symbolism in which this highly specialized creative mysticism is clothed makes for incredulity and rejection among most modern readers. I have been shown pictures which would seem pornographic but have been dignified by alchemical interpretation. The copulation of two persons, for instance, may be interpreted as the sun and moon, the male and female principles, performing the acts of primal procreation. To this may be added a complicated colour symbolism and an insistence upon water, mountains and other solitary locations. The interpretation of this alchemical art lay outside the knowledge and grasp of the Canon's Yeoman as of most people at the present time.

The modern reader is glad that Chaucer likewise eschewed it. The Yeoman's knowledge of the practical matters is not perfect (he uses the term *bole Armoniak* instead of the more correct *bolus Armenius*, for instance) and his study of such metals as arsenic and mercury was deficient. Whether these errors in the tale were genuine and unintentional or dramatically imputed to the Yeoman can hardly be decided.

From his knowledge of the grotesqueries of the world of the alchemist he was able to produce a poem that fooled Elias Ashmole, a seventeenth-century historian of alchemy, into claiming him a devotee of Hermes, the originator of magical philosophy. Chaucer might have sooner accepted Ashmole's further judgement that the poem illustrated a more popular human delusion: 'Let philosophers say what they can and wise men give never so good Counsell, no warning will serve, they must be couzened [cheated], nay they have a greedy appetite thereunto; but it has ever been so.' (*Theatrum Chemicum*, 1651). It may have been wide reading or even personal experimentation that equipped Chaucer to write the poem; it may have been a new twist to the theme of exploitation and confidence-trickery that led him to do some special research for it: we cannot tell. There is little doubt, though, that he was fully justified in allowing an intruder into the fold of the Canterbury pilgrims to tell this story.

NOTE ON THE TEXT

The text which follows is based upon that of F. N. Robinson (*The Complete Works of Geoffrey Chaucer*, 2nd ed., 1957). The punctuation has been revised, with special reference to the exclamation marks. Spelling has been partly rationalized, by substituting *i* for *y* wherever the change does not affect the semantic value of the word. Thus *smylyng* becomes 'smiling', and *nyghtyngale* 'nightingale', but *wyn* (wine), *lyk* (like), and *fyr* (fire) are allowed to stand.

No accentuation has been provided in this text, for two reasons. First, because it produces a page displeasing to the eye; secondly, because it no longer seems necessary or entirely reliable in the light of modern scholarship. It is not now thought that the later works of Chaucer were written in a ten-syllable line from which no variation was permissible. The correct reading of a line of Chaucer is now seen to be more closely related to the correct reading of a comparable line of prose with phrasing suited to the rhythms of speech. This allows the reader to be more flexible in his interpretation of the line, and makes it unreasonably pedantic to provide a rigid system of accentuation.

NOTE ON PRONUNCIATION

These equivalences are intended to offer only a rough guide. For further detail, see Hussey, Spearing and Winny, *An Introduction to Chaucer* (Chapter 4).

SHORT VOWELS

ă represents the sound now written *u*, as in 'cut'

ĕ as in modern 'set'

ĭ as in modern 'is'

ŏ as in modern 'top'

ŭ as in modern 'put' (not as in 'cut')

final *-e* represents the neutral vowel sound in '*a*bout' or 'atten*tion*'. It is silent when the next word in the line begins with a vowel or an *h*.

Note on the Text

LONG VOWELS

ā as in modern 'car' (not as in 'name')

ē (open—i.e. where the equivalent modern word is spelt with *ea*) as in modern 'there'

ē (close—i.e. where the equivalent modern word is spelt with *ee* or *e*) represents the sound now written *a* as in 'take'

ī as in modern 'machine' (not as in 'like')

ō (open—i.e. where the equivalent modern vowel is pronounced as in 'brother', 'mood', or 'good') represents the sound now written *aw* as in 'fawn'

ō (close—i.e. where the equivalent modern vowel is pronounced as in 'road') as in modern 'note'

ū as in French *tu* or German *Tür*

DIPHTHONGS

ai and *ei* both roughly represent the sound now written *i* or *y* as in 'die' or 'dye'

au and *aw* both represent the sound now written *ow* or *ou* as in 'now' or 'pounce'

ou and *ow* have two pronunciations: as in *through* where the equivalent modern vowel is pronounced as in 'through' or 'mouse'; and as in *pounce* where the equivalent modern vowel is pronounced as in 'know' or 'thought'

WRITING OF VOWELS AND DIPHTHONGS

A long vowel is often indicated by doubling, as in *roote* or *eek*. The *ŭ* sound is sometimes represented by an *o* as in *yong*. The *au* sound is sometimes represented by an *a*, especially before *m* or *n*, as in *cha(u)mbre* or *cha(u)nce*.

CONSONANTS

Largely as in modern English, except that many consonants now silent were still pronounced. *Gh* was pronounced as in Scottish 'lo*ch*', and both consonants should be pronounced in such groups as the following: '*gn*acchen', '*kn*ave', 'wor*d*', 'fo*lk*', '*wr*ong'.

THE CANON'S YEOMAN'S PROLOGUE

Whan ended was the lyf of Seinte Cecile,
Er we hadde riden fully five mile,
At Boghtoun under Blee us gan atake
A man that clothed was in clothes blake,
And under-nethe he hadde a whit surplis.
His hakeney, that was al pomely gris,
So swatte that it wonder was to see;
It semed as he had priked miles three.
The hors eek that his yeman rood upon
So swatte that unnethe mighte it gon.   10
Aboute the peytrel stood the foom ful hie;
He was of foom al flekked as a pie.
A male tweyfoold on his croper lay;
It semed that he caried lite array.
Al light for somer rood this worthy man,
And in myn herte wondren I bigan
What that he was, til that I understood
How that his cloke was sowed to his hood;
For which, whan I hadde longe avised me,
I demed him som chanoun for to be.   20
His hat heeng at his bak doun by a laas,
For he hadde riden moore than trot or paas;
He hadde ay priked like as he were wood.
A clote-leef he hadde under his hood
For swoot, and for to keep his heed from heete.
But it was joye for to seen him swete!
His forheed dropped as a stillatorie,

Were ful of plantaine and of paritorie.
And whan that he was come, he gan to crye,
30 'God save,' quod he, 'this joly compaignye!
Faste have I priked,' quod he, 'for youre sake,
By cause that I wolde yow atake,
To riden in this myrie compaignye.'
His yeman eek was ful of curteisye,
And seyde, 'Sires, now in the morwe-tide
Out of youre hostelrie I saugh yow ride,
And warned heer my lord and my soverayn,
Which that to riden with yow is ful fain
For his desport; he loveth daliaunce.'
    'Freend, for thy warning God yeve thee good
40   chaunce'
Thanne seyde oure Hoost, 'for certein it wolde
        seme
Thy lord were wys, and so I may wel deme.
He is ful jocunde also, dar I leye,
Can he oght telle a myrie tale or tweye,
With which he glade may this compaignye?'
    'Who, sire? my lord? ye, ye, withouten lie,
He kan of murthe and eek of jolitee
Nat but ynough; also, sire, trusteth me,
And ye him knewe as wel as do I,
50 Ye wolde wondre how wel and craftily
He koude werke, and that in sondry wise.
He hath take on him many a greet emprise,
Which were ful hard for any that is heere
To bringe aboute, but they of him it leere.
As hoomly as he rit amonges yow,
If ye him knewe, it wolde be for youre prow.
Ye wolde nat forgoon his aqueyntaunce

26

For muchel good, I dar leye in balaunce
Al that I have in my possessioun.
He is a man of heigh discrecioun;   60
I warne yow wel, he is a passing man.'
  'Wel,' quod oure Hoost, 'I pray thee, tel me
    than,
Is he a clerk, or noon? Telle what he is.'
  'Nay, he is gretter than a clerk, iwis,'
Seyde this Yeman, 'and in wordes fewe,
Hoost, of his craft somwhat I wol yow shewe.

  I seye, my lord kan swich subtilitee—
But al his craft ye may nat wite at me,
And somwhat helpe I yet to his wirking—
That al this ground on which we been riding,   70
Til that we come to Caunterbury toun,
He koude al clene turne it up-so-doun,
And pave it al of silver and of gold.'

  And whan this Yeman hadde this tale ytold
Unto oure Hoost, he seyde, '*Benedicitee*,
This thing is wonder merveillous to me,
Sin that thy lord is of so heigh prudence,
By cause of which men sholde him reverence,
That of his worshipe rekketh he so lite.
His overslope nis nat worth a mite,   80
As in effect, to him, so moot I go!
It is al baudy and totore also.

Why is thy lord so sluttissh, I the preye,
And is of power bettre clooth to beye,
If that his dede accorde with thy speche?
Telle me that, and that I thee biseche.'
  'Why?' quod this Yeman, 'wherto axe ye me?
God help me so, for he shal nevere thee

(But I wol nat avowe that I seye,
90   And therfore keepe it secree, I yow preye).
He is to wys, in feith, as I bileeve.
That that is overdoon, it wol nat preeve
Aright, as clerkes seyn; it is a vice.
Wherfore in that I holde him lewed and nice.
For whan a man hath over-greet a wit,
Ful oft him happeth to misusen it.
So dooth my lord, and that me greveth soore;
God it amende, I kan sey yow namoore.'
      'Ther-of no fors, good Yeman,' quod our Hoost;
100 'Sin of the konning of thy lord thow woost,
Telle how he dooth, I pray thee hertely,
Sin that he is so crafty and so sly.
Where dwelle ye, if it to telle be?'
      'In the suburbes of a toun,' quod he,
'Lurkinge in hernes and in lanes blinde,
Whereas thise robbours and thise theves by kinde
Holden hir privee fereful residence,
As they that dar nat shewen hir presence;
So faren we, if I shal seye the sothe.'
110 'Now,' quod oure Hoost, 'yit lat me talke to the.
Why artow so discoloured of thy face?'
      'Peter,' quod he, 'God yeve it harde grace,
I am so used in the fyr to blowe
That it hath chaunged my colour, I trowe.
I am nat wont in no mirour to prie,
But swinke soore and lerne multiplie.
We blondren evere and pouren in the fir,
And for al that we faille of oure desir,
For evere we lakken oure conclusioun.
120 To muchel folk we doon illusioun,

28

And borwe gold, be it a pound or two,
Or ten, or twelve, or manye sommes mo,
And make hem wenen, at the leeste weye,
That of a pound we koude make tweye.
Yet is it fals, but ay we han good hope
It for to doon, and after it we grope.
But that science is so fer us biforn,
We mowen nat, although we hadden it sworn,
It overtake, it slit awey so faste.
It wole us maken beggers atte laste.'   130

   Whil this Yeman was thus in his talking,
This Chanoun drough him neer, and herde al thing
Which that this Yeman spak, for suspecioun
Of mennes speche evere hadde this Chanoun.
For Catoun seith that he that gilty is
Demeth alle thing be spoke of him, iwis.
That was the cause he gan so ny him drawe
To his Yeman, to herknen al his sawe.
And thus he seyde unto his Yeman tho:
'Hoold thou thy pees, and spek no wordes mo,   140
For if thou do, thou shalt it deere abye.
Thou sclaundrest me heere in this compaignye,
And eek discoverest that thou sholdest hide.'

   'Ye,' quod oure Hoost, 'telle on, what so bitide.
Of al his threting rekke nat a mite.'

   'In feith,' quod he, 'namoore I do but lite.'

   And whan this Chanon saugh it wolde nat bee,
But his Yeman wolde telle his privetee,
He fledde awey for verray sorwe and shame.

   'A,' quod the Yeman, 'heere shal arise game;   150
Al that I kan anon now wol I telle.
Sin he is goon, the foule feend him quelle!

29

For nevere heerafter wol I with him meete
For peny ne for pound, I yow biheete.
He that me broghte first unto that game,
Er that he die, sorwe have he and shame
For it is ernest to me, by my feith;
That feele I wel, what so any man seith.
And yet, for al my smert and al my grief,
For al my sorwe, labour, and meschief,
I koude nevere leve it in no wise.
Now wolde God my wit mighte suffise
To tellen al that longeth to that art
But nathelees yow wol I tellen part.
Sin that my lord is goon, I wol nat spare;
Swich thing as that I knowe, I wol declare.

   With this Chanoun I dwelt have seven yeer,
And of his science am I never the neer.
Al that I hadde I have lost therby,
And, God woot, so hath many mo than I.
Ther I was wont to be right fressh and gay
Of clothing and of oother good array,
Now may I were an hose upon myn heed;
And wher my colour was bothe fressh and reed,
Now is it wan and of a leden hewe—
Whoso it useth, soore shal he rewe—
And of my swink yet blered is myn ye.
Lo! which avantage is to multiplie!
That slidinge science hath me maad so bare
That I have no good, wher that evere I fare;
And yet I am endetted so therby,
Of gold that I have borwed, trewely,
That whil I live I shal it quite nevere.
Lat every man be war by me for evere

160

170

180

What maner man that casteth him therto,
If he continue, I holde his thrift ydo.
For so helpe me God, therby shal he nat winne,
But empte his purs, and make his wittes thinne.
And whan he, thurgh his madnesse and folye,
Hath lost his owene good thurgh jupartye,   190
Thanne he exciteth oother folk therto,
To lesen hir good, as he himself hath do.
For unto shrewes joye it is and ese
To have hir felawes in peyne and disese.
Thus was I ones lerned of a clerk.
Of that no charge, I wol speke of oure werk.

  Whan we been there as we shul exercise
Oure elvisshe craft, we semen wonder wise,
Oure termes been so clergial and so queynte.
I blowe the fir til that myn herte feynte.   200
What sholde I tellen ech proporcion
Of thinges whiche that we werche upon—
As on five or sixe ounces, may wel be,
Of silver, or som oother quantitee—
And bisye me to telle yow the names
Of orpiment, brent bones, iren squames,
That into poudre grounden been ful smal;
And in an erthen pot how put is al,
And salt yput in, and also papeer,
Biforn thise poudres that I speke of heer;   210
And wel ycovered with a lampe of glas;
And of muche oother thing which that ther was;
And of the pot and glasses enluting,
That of the eyr mighte passe out nothing;
And of the esy fir, and smart also,
Which that was maad, and of the care and wo

That we hadde in oure matires subliming,
And in amalgaming and calcening
Of quiksilver, yclept mercurie crude?
220   For alle oure sleightes we kan nat conclude.
Oure orpiment and sublimed mercurie,
Oure grounden litarge eek on the porfurie,
Of ech of thise of ounces a certeyn—
Noght helpeth us, oure labour is in veyn.
Ne eek oure spirites ascencioun,
Ne oure materes that lien al fix adoun,
Mowe in oure werking no thing us availle,
For lost is al oure labour and travaille;
And al the cost, a twenty devel waye,
230   Is lost also, which we upon it laye.

    Ther is also ful many another thing
That is unto oure craft apertening.
Though I by ordre hem nat reherce kan,
By cause that I am a lewed man,
Yet wol I telle hem as they come to minde,
Thogh I ne kan nat sette hem in hir kinde:
As boole armoniak, verdegrees, boras,
And sondry vessels maad of erthe and glas,
Oure urinales and oure descensories,
240   Violes, crosletz, and sublimatories,
Cucurbites and alambikes eek,
And othere swiche, deere ynough a leek,
Nat nedeth it for to reherce hem alle,—
Watres rubifying, and boles galle,
Arsenik, sal armoniak, and brimstoon;
And herbes koude I telle eek many oon,
As egremoine, valerian, and lunarie,
And othere swiche, if that me liste tarie;

Oure lampes brenning bothe night and day,
To bringe aboute oure purpos, if we may;   250
Oure fourneys eek of calcinacioun,
And of watres albificacioun;
Unslekked lim, chalk, and gleyre of an ey,
Poudres diverse, asshes, donge, pisse, and cley,
Cered pokkets, sal peter, vitriole,
And diverse fires maad of wode and cole;
Sal tartre, alkaly, and sal preparat,
And combust materes and coagulat;
Cley maad with hors or mannes heer, and oille
Of tartre, alum glas, berme, wort, and argoille,   260
Resalgar, and oure materes enbibing,
And eek of oure materes encorporing,
And of oure silver citrinacioun,
Oure cementing and fermentacioun,
Oure ingottes, testes, and many mo.

   I wol yow telle, as was me taught also,
The foure spirites and the bodies sevene,
By ordre, as ofte I herde my lord hem nevene.

   The firste spirit quiksilver called is,
The seconde orpiment, the thridde, iwis,   270
Sal armoniak, and the ferthe brimstoon.
The bodies sevene eek, lo! hem heere anoon:
Sol gold is, and Luna silver we threpe,
Mars iren, Mercurie quiksilver we clepe,
Saturnus leed, and Juppiter is tin,
And Venus coper, by my fader kin.

   This cursed craft whoso wole excercise,
He shal no good han that him may suffise;
For al the good he spendeth theraboute
He lese shal; therof have I no doute.   280

Whoso that listeth outen his folie,
Lat him come forth and lerne multiplie;
And every man that oght hath in his cofre,
Lat him appiere, and wexe a philosophre.
Ascaunce that craft is so light to leere?
Nay, nay, God woot, al be he monk or frere,
Preest or chanoun, or any oother wight,
Though he sitte at his book bothe day and night
In lerning of this elvisshe nice loore,
290   Al is in veyn, and parde, muchel moore.
To lerne a lewed man this subtiltee—
Fy, spek nat therof, for it wol nat bee;
And konne he letterure, or konne he noon,
As in effect, he shal finde it al oon.
For bothe two, by my savacioun,
Concluden in multiplicacioun
Ylike wel, whan they han al ydo;
This is to seyn, they faillen bothe two.

    Yet forgat I to maken rehersaille
300   Of watres corosif, and of lemaille,
And of bodies mollificacioun,
And also of hire induracioun;
Oilles, ablucions, and metal fusible,—
To tellen al wolde passen any bible
That owher is; wherfore, as for the beste,
Of alle thise names now wol I me reste.
For, as I trowe, I have yow toold ynowe
To reyse a feend, al looke he never so rowe.

    A nay, lat be; the philosophres stoon,
310   Elixer clept, we sechen faste echoon;
For hadde we him, thanne were we siker ynow.
But unto God of hevene I make avow,

34

For al oure craft, whan we han al ydo,
And al oure sleighte, he wol nat come us to.
He hath ymaad us spenden muchel good,
For sorwe of which almoost we wexen wood,
But that good hope crepeth in oure herte,
Supposinge evere, though we sore smerte,
To be releeved by him afterward.
Swich supposing and hope is sharp and hard;   320
I warne yow wel, it is to seken evere.
That futur temps hath maad men to dissevere,
In trust therof, from al that evere they hadde.
Yet of that art they kan nat wexen sadde,
For unto hem it is a bitter sweete,—
So semeth it,—for nadde they but a sheete,
Which that they mighte wrappe hem inne a-night,
And a brat to walken inne by daylight,
They wolde hem selle and spenden on this craft.
They kan nat stinte til no thing be laft.   330
And everemoore, where that evere they goon,
Men may hem knowe by smel of brimstoon.
For al the world they stinken as a goot;
Hir savour is so rammissh and so hoot
That though a man from hem a mile be,
The savour wole infecte him, trusteth me.
And thus by smel, and by threedbare array,
If that men liste, this folk they knowe may.
And if a man wole aske hem prively
Why they been clothed so unthriftily,   340
They right anon wol rownen in his ere,
And seyn that if that they espied were,
Men wolde hem slee by cause of hir science.
Lo, thus this folk bitrayen innocence.

Passe over this; I go my tale unto.
Er that the pot be on the fir ydo,
Of metals with a certeyn quantitee,
My lord hem tempreth, and no man but he—
Now he is goon, I dar seyn boldely—
350   For, as men seyn, he kan doon craftily.
Algate I woot wel he hath swich a name,
And yet ful ofte he renneth in a blame.
And wite ye how? Ful ofte it happeth so,
The pot tobreketh, and farewel, al is go!
Thise metals been of so greet violence,
Oure walles mowe nat make hem resistence,
But if they weren wroght of lim and stoon;
They percen so, and thurgh the wal they goon.
And somme of hem sinken into the ground—
360   Thus han we lost by times many a pound—
And somme are scatered al the floor aboute;
Somme lepe into the roof. Withouten doute,
Though that the feend noght in oure sighte him
      shewe,
I trowe he with us be, that ilke shrewe,
In helle, where that he lord is and sire,
Nis ther moore wo, ne moore rancour ne ire.
Whan that oure pot is broke, as I have said,
Every man chit, and halt him yvele apaid.
  Somme seyde it was long on the fir making;
370   Somme seyde nay, it was on the blowing,—
Thanne was I fered, for that was myn office.
'Straw,' quod the thridde, 'ye been lewed and nice.
It was nat tempred as it oghte be.'
'Nay,' quod the fourthe, 'stint and herkne me.
By cause oure fir ne was nat maad of beech,

36

That is the cause, and oother noon, so thee'ch.'
I kan nat telle wheron it was long,
But wel I woot greet strif is us among.
   'What,' quod my lord, 'ther is namoore to
      doone;
Of thise perils I wol be war eftsoone.   380
I am right siker that the pot was crased.
Be as be may, be ye no thing amased;
As usage is, lat swepe the floor as swithe,
Plukke up youre hertes, and beeth glad and blithe.'
   The mullok on an heep ysweped was,
And on the floor ycast a canevas,
And al this mullok in a sive ythrowe,
And sifted, and ypiked many a throwe.
   'Pardee,' quod oon, 'somwhat of oure metal
Yet is ther heere, though that we han nat al.   390
Although this thing mishapped have as now,
Another time it may be well ynow.
Us moste putte oure good in aventure.
A marchant, pardee, may nat ay endure,
Trusteth me wel, in his prosperitee.
Somtime his good is drowned in the see,
And somtime comth it sauf unto the londe.'
   'Pees,' quod my lord, 'the nexte time I wol fonde
To bringen oure craft al in another plite,
And but I do, sires, lat me han the wite.   400
Ther was defaute in somwhat, wel I woot.'
   Another seyde the fir was over-hoot,—
But, be it hoot or coold, I dar seye this,
That we concluden everemoore amys.
We faille of that which that we wolden have,
And in oure madnesse everemoore we rave.

And whan we been togidres everichoon,
Every man semeth a Salomon.
But al thing which that shineth as the gold
410   Nis nat gold, as that I have herd it told;
Ne every appul that is fair at eye
Ne is nat good, what so men clappe or crye.
Right so, lo, fareth it amonges us:
He that semeth the wiseste, by Jhesus!
Is moost fool, whan it cometh to the preef;
And he that semeth trewest is a theef.
That shul ye knowe, er that I fro yow wende,
By that I of my tale have maad an ende.

THE CANON'S YEOMAN'S
TALE

Ther is a chanoun of religioun
Amonges us, wolde infecte al a toun,   420
Thogh it as greet were as was Ninivee,
Rome, Alisaundre, Troye, and othere three.
His sleightes and his infinite falsnesse
Ther koude no man writen, as I gesse,
Though that he mighte live a thousand yeer.
In al this world of falshede nis his peer;
For in his termes he wol him so winde,
And speke his wordes in so sly a kinde,
Whanne he commune shal with any wight,
That he wol make him doten anonright,   430
But it a feend be, as himselven is.
Ful many a man hath he bigiled er this,
And wole, if that he live may a while;
And yet men ride and goon ful many a mile
Him for to seke and have his aqueyntaunce,
Noght knowinge of his false governaunce.
And if yow list to yeve me audience,
I wol it tellen heere in youre presence.
    But, worshipful chanons religious,
Ne demeth nat that I sclaundre youre hous,   440
Although that my tale of a chanoun bee;
Of every ordre som shrewe is, pardee,
And God forbede that al a compaignye
Sholde rewe o singuleer mannes folye.
To sclaundre yow is no thing myn entente,

39

But to correcten that is mis I mente.
This tale was nat oonly toold for yow,
But eek for othere mo; ye woot wel how
That among Cristes apostelles twelve
450 Ther nas no traitour but Judas himselve.
Thanne why sholde al the remenant have a blame
That giltlees were? By yow I seye the same,
Save oonly this, if ye wol herkne me:
If any Judas in youre covent be,
Remoeveth him bitimes, I yow rede,
If shame or los may causen any drede.
And beeth no thing displesed, I yow preye,
But in this cas herkneth what I shal seye.

In Londoun was a preest, an annueleer,
460 That therinne dwelled hadde many a yeer,
Which was so plesaunt and so servisable
Unto the wyf, where as he was at table,
That she wolde suffre him no thing for to paye
For bord ne clothing, wente he never so gaye;
And spending silver hadde he right ynow.
Therof no fors; I wol procede as now,
And telle forth my tale of the chanoun
That broghte this preest to confusioun.

This false chanon cam upon a day
470 Unto this preestes chambre, wher he lay,
Bisechinge him to lene him a certeyn
Of gold, and he wolde quite it him ageyn.
'Leene me a marc,' quod he, 'but dayes three,
And at my day I wol it quiten thee.
And if so be that thow me finde fals,
Another day do hange me by the hals.'

This preest him took a marc, and that as swithe,

And this chanoun him thanked ofte sithe,
And took his leve, and wente forth his weye,
And at the thridde day broghte his moneye,   480
And to the preest he took his gold agayn,
Wherof this preest was wonder glad and fayn.

  'Certes,' quod he, 'no thing anoyeth me
To lene a man a noble, or two, or thre,
Or what thing were in my possessioun,
Whan he so trewe is of condicioun
That in no wise he breke wole his day;
To swich a man I kan never seye nay.'

  'What,' quod this chanoun, 'sholde I be
    untrewe?
Nay, that were thing yfallen al of newe.   490
Trouthe is a thing that I wol evere kepe
Unto that day in which that I shal crepe
Into my grave, and ellis God forbede.
Bileveth this as siker as your Crede.
God thanke I, and in good time be it said,
That ther was nevere man yet yvele apaid
For gold ne silver that he to me lente,
Ne nevere falshede in min herte I mente.
And sire,' quod he, 'now of my privetee,
Sin ye so goodlich han been unto me,   500
And kithed to me so greet gentillesse,
Somwhat to quite with youre kindenesse
I wol yow shewe, and if yow list to leere,
I wol yow teche pleynly the manere
How I kan werken in philosophie.
Taketh good heede, ye shul wel seen at yë
That I wol doon a maistrie er I go.'

  'Ye,' quod the preest, 'ye, sire, and wol ye so?

Marie, therof I pray yow hertely.'
510   'At youre comandement, sire, trewely,'
Quod the chanoun, 'and ellis God forbeede.'
    Loo, how this theef koude his service beede!
Ful sooth it is that swich profred servise
Stinketh, as witnessen thise olde wise,
And that, ful soone I wol it verifie
In this chanoun, roote of al trecherie,
That everemoore delit hath and gladnesse—
Swiche feendly thoghtes in his herte impresse—
How Cristes peple he may to meschief bringe.
520 God kepe us from his false dissimulinge.
    Noght wiste this preest with whom that he delte,
Ne of his harm cominge he no thing felte.
O sely preest, o sely innocent,
With coveitise anon thou shalt be blent.
O gracelees, ful blind is thy conceite,
No thing ne artow war of the deceite
Which that this fox yshapen hath to thee.
His wily wrenches thou ne mayst nat flee.
Wherfore, to go to the conclusion,
530 That refereth to thy confusion,
Unhappy man, anon I wol me hie
To tellen thyn unwit and thy folye,
And eek the falsnesse of that oother wrecche,
As ferforth as that my konning wol strecche.
    This chanon was my lord, ye wolden weene?
Sire hoost, in feith, and by the hevenes queene,
It was another chanoun, and nat hee,
That kan an hundred foold moore subtiltee.
He hath bitrayed folkes many time;
540 Of his falsnesse it dulleth me to rime.

42

Evere whan that I speke of his falshede,
For shame of him my chekes wexen rede.
Algates they biginnen for to glowe,
For reednesse have I noon, right wel I knowe,
In my visage; for fumes diverse
Of metals, whiche ye han herd me reherce,
Consumed and wasted han my reednesse.
Now taak heede of this chanons cursednesse.

  'Sire,' quod he to the preest, 'lat youre man gon
For quiksilver, that we it hadde anon;   550
And lat him bringen ounces two or three;
And whan he comth, as faste shal ye see
A wonder thing, which ye saugh nevere er this.'

  'Sire,' quod the preest, 'it shal be doon, iwis.'
He bad his servant fecchen him this thing,
And he al redy was at his bidding,
And wente him forth, and cam anon again
With this quiksilver, shortly for to sayn,
And took thise ounces thre to the chanoun;
And he hem leyde faire and wel adoun,   560
And bad the servant coles for to bringe,
That he anon mighte go to his werkinge.

  The coles right anon weren yfet,
And this chanoun took out a crosselet
Of his bosom, and shewed it to the preest.
'This instrument,' quod he, 'which that thou seest,
Taak in thyn hand, and put thyself therinne
Of this quiksilver an ounce, and heer biginne,
In name of Crist, to wexe a philosofre.
Ther been ful fewe to whiche I wolde profre   570
To shewen hem thus muche of my science.
For ye shul seen heer, by experience,

That this quiksilver I wol mortifye
Right in youre sighte anon, withouten lie,
And make it as good silver and as fyn
As ther is any in youre purs or myn,
Or elleswhere, and make it malliable;
And elles holdeth me fals and unable
Amonges folk for evere to appeere.
580 I have a poudre heer, that coste me deere,
Shal make al good, for it is cause of al
My konning, which that I yow shewen shal.
Voide youre man, and lat him be theroute,
And shette the dore, whils we been aboute
Oure privetee, that no man us espie,
Whils that we werke in this philosophie.'

Al as he bad fulfilled was in dede.
This ilke servant anonright out yede
And his maister shette the dore anon,
590 And to hire labour spedily they gon.

This preest, at this cursed chanons bidding,
Upon the fir anon sette this thing,
And blew the fir, and bisied him ful faste.
And this chanoun into the crosselet caste
A poudre, noot I wherof that it was
Ymaad, outher of chalk, outher of glas,
Or somwhat elles, was nat worth a flye,
To blinde with this preest; and bad him hie
The coles for to couchen al above
600 The crosselet. 'For in tokening I thee love,'
Quod this chanoun, 'thine owene handes two
Shul werche al thing which that shal heer be do.'

'Graunt mercy,' quod the preest, and was ful
    glad,

44

And couched coles as that the chanoun bad.
And while he bisy was, this feendly wrecche,
This false chanoun—the foule feend him fecche—
Out of his bosom took a bechen cole,
In which ful subtilly was maad an hole,
And therinne put was of silver lemaille
An ounce, and stopped was, withouten faille,   610
This hole with wex, to kepe the lemaille in.
And understondeth that this false gin
Was nat maad ther, but it was maad bifore;
And othere thinges I shal tellen moore
Herafterward, whiche that he with him broghte.
Er he cam there, him to bigile he thoghte,
And so he dide, er that they wente atwinne;
Til he had terved him, koude he nat blinne.
It dulleth me whan that I of him speke.
On his falshede fain wolde I me wreke,   620
If I wiste how, but he is heere and there;
He is so variaunt, he abit nowhere.

But taketh heede now, sires, for Goddes love,
He took his cole of which I spak above,
And in his hand he baar it prively.
And whiles the preest couched bisily
The coles, as I tolde yow er this,
This chanoun seyde, 'Freend, ye doon amis.
This is nat couched as it oghte be;
But soone I shal amenden it,' quod he.   630
'Now lat me medle therwith but a while,
For of yow have I pitee, by Seint Gile,
Ye been right hoot; I se wel how ye swete.
Have heere a clooth, and wipe awey the wete.'
And whiles that the preest wiped his face,

45

This chanoun took his cole—with sory grace—
And leyde it above upon the middeward
Of the crosselet, and blew wel afterward,
Til that the coles gonne faste brenne.
640   'Now yeve us drinke,' quod the chanoun thenne;
'As swithe al shal be wel, I undertake.
Sitte we doun, and lat us myrie make.'
And whan that this chanounes bechen cole
Was brent, al the lemaille out of the hole
Into the crosselet fil anon adoun;
And so it moste nedes, by resoun,
Sin it so evene aboven it couched was.
But therof wiste the preest nothing, alas!
He demed alle the coles yliche good;
650 For of that sleighte he nothing understood.
And whan this alkamistre saugh his time,
'Ris up,' quod he, 'sire preest, and stondeth by me;
And for I woot wel ingot have ye noon,
Gooth, walketh forth, and bringe us a chalk stoon;
For I wol make it of the same shap
That is an ingot, if I may han hap.
And bringeth eek with yow a bolle or a panne
Ful of water, and ye shul se wel thanne
How that oure bisinesse shal thrive and preeve.
660 And yet, for ye shul han no misbileeve
Ne wrong conceite of me in youre absence,
I ne wol nat been out of youre presence,
But go with yow, and come with yow ageyn.'
The chambre dore, shortly for to seyn,
They opened and shette, and wente hir weye.
And forth with hem they carieden the keye,
And coome again withouten any delay.

46

What sholde I tarien al the longe day?
He took the chalk, and shoop it in the wise
Of an ingot, as I shal yow devise.   670

  I seye, he took out of his owene sleeve
A teyne of silver—yvele moot he cheeve—
Which that ne was nat but an ounce of weighte.
And taaketh heede now of his cursed sleighte.

  He shoop his ingot, in lengthe and in breede
Of this teyne, withouten any drede,
So slily that the preest it nat espide,
And in his sleve again he gan it hide,
And fro the fir he took up his mateere,
And in th'ingot putte it with myrie cheere,   680
And in the water-vessel he it caste,
Whan that him luste, and bad the preest as faste,
'Loke what ther is, put in thyn hand and grope.
Thow finde shalt ther silver, as I hope.'
What, devel of helle, sholde it elles be?
Shaving of silver silver is, pardee.
He putte his hand in and took up a teyne
Of silver fyn, and glad in every veyne
Was this preest, whan he saugh that it was so.
'Goddes blessing, and his moodres also,   690
And alle halwes, have ye, sire chanoun,'
Seyde the preest, 'and I hir malisoun,
But, and ye vouche-sauf to techen me
This noble craft and this subtilitee,
I wol be youre in al that evere I may.'

  Quod the chanoun, 'Yet wol I make assay
The seconde time, that ye may taken heede
And been expert of this, and in youre neede
Another day assaye in myn absence

700 This discipline and this crafty science.
Lat take another ounce,' quod he tho,
'Of quiksilver, withouten wordes mo,
And do therwith as ye han doon er this
With that oother, which that now silver is.'
    This preest him bisieth in al that he kan
To doon as this chanoun, this cursed man,
Comanded him, and faste he blew the fir,
For to come to th'effect of his desir.
And this chanon, right in the meene while,
710 Al redy was this preest eft to bigile,
And for a contenaunce in his hand he bar
An holwe stikke—taak kep and be war—
In the ende of which an ounce, and namoore,
Of silver lemaille put was, as bifore
Was in his cole, and stopped with wex weel
For to kepe in his lemaille every deel.
And whil this preest was in his bisynesse,
This chanoun with his stikke gan him dresse
To him anon, and his poudre caste in
720 As he dide er—the devel out of his skin
Him terve, I pray to God, for his falshede,
For he was evere fals in thoght and dede—
And with this stikke, above the crosselet,
That was ordeyned with that false jet
He stired the coles til relente gan
The wex again the fir, as every man,
But it a fool be, woot wel it moot nede,
And al that in the stikke was out yede,
And in the crosselet hastily it fel.
730   Now, good sires, what wol ye bet than wel?
Whan that this preest thus was bigiled ageyn,

48

Supposinge noght but treuthe, sooth to seyn,
He was so glad that I kan nat expresse
In no manere his mirthe and his gladnesse;
And to the chanoun he profred eftsoone
Body and good. 'Ye,' quod the chanoun soone,
'Though poure I be, crafty thou shalt me finde.
I warne thee, yet is ther moore bihinde.
Is ther any coper herinne?' seyde he.

   'Ye,' quod the preest, 'sire, I trowe wel ther be.' 740
   'Elles go bye us som, and that as swithe;
Now, goode sire, go forth thy wey and hie the.'

   He wente his wey, and with the coper cam,
And this chanon it in his handes nam,
And of that coper weyed out but an ounce.

   Al to simple is my tonge to pronounce,
As ministre of my wit, the doublenesse
Of this chanoun, roote of alle cursednesse,
He semed freendly to hem that knewe him noght,
But he was feendly bothe in werk and thoght. 750
It weerieth me to telle of his falsnesse,
And nathelees yet wol I it expresse,
To th'entente that men may be war therby,
And for noon oother cause, trewely.

   He putte this ounce of coper in the crosselet,
And on the fir as swithe he hath it set,
And caste in poudre, and made the preest to blowe,
And in his werking for to stoupe lowe,
As he dide er,—and al nas but a jape;
Right as him liste, the preest he made his ape, 760
And afterward in the ingot he it caste,
And in the panne putte it at the laste
Of water, and in he putte his owene hand,

And in his sleve (as ye biforen-hand
Herde me telle) he hadde a silver teyne.
He slily took it out, this cursed heyne,
Unwiting this preest of his false craft,
And in the pannes botme he hath it laft;
And in the water rombled to and fro,
770   And wonder prively took up also
The coper teyne, noght knowinge this preest,
And hidde it, and him hente by the breest,
And to him spak, and thus seyde in his game:
'Stoupeth adoun, by God, ye be to blame,
Helpeth me now, as I dide yow whileer;
Putte in youre hand, and looketh what is theer.'

    This preest took up this silver teyne anon,
And thanne seyde the chanoun, 'Lat us gon
With thise thre teynes, whiche that we han wroght,
780   To som goldsmith, and wite if they been oght.
For, by my feith, I nolde, for myn hood,
But if that they were silver fin and good,
And that as swithe preeved it shal bee.'

    Unto the goldsmith with thise teynes three
They wente, and putte thise teynes in assay
To fir and hamer; mighte no man seye nay,
But that they weren as hem oghte be.

    This sotted preest, who was gladder than he?
Was nevere brid gladder again the day,
790   Ne nightingale, in the sesoun of May,
Was nevere noon that luste bet to singe;
Ne lady lustier in carolinge,
Or for to speke of love and wommanhede,
Ne knight in armes to doon an hardy dede,
To stonden in grace of his lady deere,

Than hadde this preest this soory craft to leere.
And to the chanoun thus he spak and seyde:
'For love of God, that for us alle deyde,
And as I may deserve it unto yow,
What shal this receite coste? telleth now.'   800
   'By oure Lady,' quod this chanoun, 'it is deere,
I warne yow wel; for save I and a frere,
In Engelond ther kan no man it make.'
   'No fors,' quod he, 'now, sire, for Goddes sake,
What shal I paye? Telleth me, I preye.'
   'Ywis,' quod he, 'it is ful deere, I seye.
Sire, at o word, if that thee list it have,
Ye shul paye fourty pound, so God me save.
And nere the freendshipe that ye dide er this
To me, ye sholde paye moore, ywis.'   810
   This preest the somme of fourty pound anon
Of nobles fette, and took hem everichon
To this chanoun, for this ilke receite.
Al his werking nas but fraude and deceite.
   'Sire preest,' he seyde, 'I kepe han no loos
Of my craft, for I wolde it kept were cloos;
And, as ye love me, kepeth it secree.
For, and men knewen al my soutiltee,
By God, they wolden han so greet envye
To me, by cause of my philosophye,   820
I sholde be deed; ther were noon oother weye.'
   'God it forbeede,' quod the preest, 'what sey ye?
Yet hadde I levere spenden al the good
Which that I have, and elles wexe I wood,
Than that ye sholden falle in swich mescheef'
   'For youre good wil, sire, have ye right good
      preef,'

Quod the chanoun, 'and farwel, grant mercy.'
He wente his wey, and never the preest him sy
After that day; and whan that this preest shoolde
830   Maken assay, at swich time as he wolde,
Of this receit, farwel, it wolde nat be.
Lo, thus bijaped and bigiled was he!
Thus maketh he his introduccioun,
To bringe folk to hir destruccioun.

    Considereth, sires, how that, in ech estaat,
Bitwixe men and gold ther is debaat
So ferforth that unnethes is ther noon.
This multiplying blent so many oon
That in good feith I trowe that it bee
840   The cause grettest of swich scarsetee.
Philosophres speken so mistily
In this craft that men kan nat come therby,
For any wit that men han now-a-dayes.
They mowe wel chiteren as doon thise jayes,
And in hir termes sette hir lust and peyne,
But to hir purpos shul they nevere atteyne.
A man may lightly lerne, if he have aught,
To multiplie, and bringe his good to naught.

    Lo, swich a lucre is in this lusty game,
850   A mannes mirthe it wol turne unto grame,
And empten also grete and hevye purses,
And maken folk for to purchacen curses
Of hem that han hir good therto ylent.
O! fy, for shame, they that han been brent,
Allas, kan they nat flee the fires heete?
Ye that it use, I rede ye it leete,
Lest ye lese al; for bet than nevere is late.
Nevere to thrive were to long a date.

Though ye prolle ay, ye shul it nevere finde.
Ye been as boold as is Bayard the blinde,   860
That blondreth forth, and peril casteth noon.
He is as boold to renne again a stoon
As for to goon bisides in the weye.
So faren ye that multiplie, I seye.
If that youre eyen kan nat seen aright,
Looke that youre minde lakke noght his sight.
For though ye looken never so brode and stare,
Ye shul nothing winne on that chaffare,
But wasten al that ye may rape and renne.
Withdraweth the fir, lest it to faste brenne;   870
Medleth namoore with that art, I mene,
For if ye doon, youre thrift is goon ful clene.
And right as swithe I wol yow tellen heere
What philosophres seyn in this mateere.

   Lo, thus seith Arnold of the Newe Toun,
As his Rosarie maketh mencioun;
He seith right thus, withouten any lie:
'Ther may no man mercurie mortifie
But it be with his brother knowleching.'
How be that he which that first seyde this thing   880
Of philosophres fader was, Hermes—
He seith how that the dragon, doutelees,
Ne dieth nat, but if that he be slain
With his brother; and that is for to sayn,
By the dragon, Mercurie, and noon oother
He understood, and brimstoon by his brother,
That out of Sol and Luna were ydrawe.
'And therfore,' seyde he,—taak heede to my sawe—
'Lat no man bisye him this art for to seche,
But if that he th'entencioun and speche   890

53

Of philosophres understonde kan;
And if he do, he is a lewed man.
For this science and this konning,' quod he,
'Is of the secree of secrees, pardee.'

    Also ther was a disciple of Plato,
That on a time seyde his maister to,
As his book Senior wol bere witnesse,
And this was his demande in soothfastnesse:
'Telle me the name of the privee stoon?'

900   And Plato answerde unto him anoon,
'Take the stoon that Titanos men name.'
    'Which is that?' quod he. 'Magnasia is the
      same,'
Seyde Plato. 'Ye, sire, and is it thus?
This is *ignotum per ignocius*.
What is Magnasia, good sire, I yow preye?'
    'It is a water that is maad, I seye,
Of elementes foure,' quod Plato.
    'Telle me the roote, good sire,' quod he tho,
'Of that water, if it be youre wil.'

910   'Nay, nay,' quod Plato, 'certain, that I nil.
The philosophres sworn were everychoon
That they sholden discovere it unto noon,
Ne in no book it write in no manere.
For unto Crist it is so lief and deere
That he wol nat that it discovered bee,
But where it liketh to his deitee
Men for t'enspire, and eek for to deffende
Whom that him liketh; lo, this is the ende.'
    Thanne conclude I thus, sith that God of hevene

920 Ne wil nat that the philosophres nevene
How that a man shal come unto this stoon,

The Canon's Yeoman's Tale

I rede, as for the beste, lete it goon.
For whoso maketh God his adversarie,
As for to werken any thing in contrarie
Of his wil, certes, never shal he thrive,
Thogh that he multiplie terme of his live.
And there a point; for ended is my tale.
God sende every trewe man boote of his bale!

NOTES

1. *Seinte Cecile* The martyrdom of St Cecilia is the subject of the previous tale, the *Second Nun's*. On the question of links between the two tales see Introduction, p. 4.

3. *Boghtoun under Blee* A spot in Blean forest, about five miles from Ospringe which was a common halt for pilgrims. This is one of several hints throughout the tales of the progress of the pilgrims along the road to Canterbury.

    gan atake 'overtook'.

4. *clothes blake* Since the Canon and his Yeoman are new to the book, each is given the type of description already familiar in the *General Prologue*. The clerical profession of the alchemist becomes an important matter.

7. *swatte* The haste of the Canon's entrance and exit provides excitement in the prologue which is maintained in the tale. Men and horses are all bathed in sweat and drip like a *stillatorie*. In other words, they are being compared here with alchemical apparatus before it was even known that they followed that profession. The poetic texture and the figurative language are ahead of the concrete documentation of the story which is still to come.

13. *male tweyfoold* If his bag doubled over very easily it was virtually empty. He is either presented as short of money or else as travelling light and ready to flit. A man like the Host might be expected to notice such details as this: innkeepers are well aware of the implications of travellers without luggage.

17–18. In the phrases *what that*, *til that* and *how that* it is necessary to suppress the redundant *that*. In French the conjunction *que* is similarly over-employed. Certain orders of canons were required to wear hoods when away from their religious houses.

24–5. The burdock leaf used to prevent sweat adds verisimilitude to the portrait. The transition to *plantaine* and *paritorie*, both employed in the processes of distillation, is a further example of the natural growth of the theme of the poem out of the images used in it: before the Canon's profession has been mentioned three specialized words have been introduced.

Notes

31. *faste have I priked* We can find no logical reason for such speed since we assume the pilgrims to have been taking their time. It may therefore be possible to interpret it as a dramatic flash, something sudden and exciting, a symbolic or poetic activity as much as a perfectly natural one.

37. *my lord and my soverayn* The speaker's courtesy becomes ironic if we recall the mouldy, dingy appearance of the Canon. It adds a flavour of confidence-trick to this section. The sales talk which the Yeoman practises recalls the confidence-trick of the Pardoner on the same group. The tone is crucial because of the effect of the Yeoman's speeches upon the Canon, but it is left to the reader to feel it and interpret it, as in reading a play.

39. *desport...daliaunce* Neither quality is appropriate to a Canon. Here the ironies begin to come to the surface and show themselves for what they are: not praise of the Canon but a criticism of him. Words like *worthy*, *konning*, *sly* and *craft* can bear both favourable and unfavourable interpretation. It is left to the reader to decide at what point he thinks the speaker passes from praise to blame. These words should therefore be carefully noted as they recur.

49. *and* 'if'. This use is often found in Elizabethan English, where it is normally written 'an'.

52. *greet emprise* Here the speaker has become insinuating, and the Canon's disappearance is well prepared. Having praised him in these terms in his presence the Yeoman then tells the truth behind his back with the same rush of emotion or absence of discretion.

55. *hoomly* 'Though he rides among you like a man of no distinction.' The simplicity of his appearance is thrown into contrast with his great knowledge and it tends to go to his discredit.

61. *passing* 'surpassing', but possibly also with a quibble on the fact that he passes so swiftly from the scene.

63. See how often the Host needles the Yeoman with his questions. Harry the Host is frequently used as a mask for Chaucer himself and appears now in the role of questioner. It is this process that we have to assume that the poet himself undertook in order to elicit information from pilgrims which was not open to observation. This is how we are to assume that Chaucer worked.

68–9. 'Even if I assist you it will not be possible for you to learn all his craft from me.' The Yeoman realizes that his rush to implicate his master looks like an admission of his own guilt. This passage suggests that the speaker is extremely unwise and indiscreet in his revelations.

73. *pave it al of silver* Though the Host is not taken in by it, the sales talk has crossed the frontier of the ridiculous.

80. *nis nat* Multiple negatives remain negative in the work of Chaucer, strengthening the meaning and not cancelling it out.

81. 'In fact his overcoat isn't worth a bean to him, as sure as I am telling you.'

82. *baudy and tortore* 'all dirty and torn in shreds'. The Host's shrewd reply undermines the effects of all the sales talk.

83. *sluttissh* The scruffiness of alchemists was traditional.

84. *and is of power* 'since he has the ability'.

88. *nevere thee* never thrive.

89. 'I cannot avouch all I have stated.'

91. *wis* either 'too philosophical to parade his wealth' or 'too shrewd to reveal his potential resources'.

92. *overdoon* 'exaggerated in show'.

93–7. 'In this I think he is being ignorant and foolish. It often happens that when a man has immense learning he contrives to misplace his enthusiasms. This is what my master does and it upsets me most severely.'

96. *misusen* The problem of the misuse of scientific insight arises here; the speaker utters a valid comment. Though the Yeoman is presented as limited in understanding, the poet has used him to convey an idea that looks almost modern to us.

99. *no fors* 'no matter'.

105. For comment upon this important passage, see p. 12.

111. *discoloured* The laboratory steward of the Middle Ages was presented as worn out with his labours and pale-faced from working with the bellows for greater and greater temperatures. The anguish and the change of colour both point towards a more deep-seated form of discomfort, a spiritual state. The discolorations of fluids and metals in the laboratory are perhaps extensions of this visual image.

112. *Peter* An oath.
    harde grace 'ill favour'.

115. *mirour* Though he is said to have no time to watch the gradual process of his discoloration he is fully aware of it.

Notes

The mirror-symbol may suggest the element of illusion that engulfs the whole process of alchemy.

116. *lerne multiplie* 'study transmutation of metals'.

117. *blondren* To be understood in two senses: (1) to go round and round in circles; (2) to blunder, to act wrongly. The Yeoman sees only the first and more external application, but the poet intends the reader to seize upon the ethical aspect. Throughout the poetry of Chaucer we come upon words that have social or physical meanings at first sight but reveal a religious or ethical purpose when they are weighed more deeply.

pouren 'gaze, pore'.

120. In this line we find the difficulties of summing up this speaker's attitude towards his career. He admits that he has been misled and has failed 'in desir' so that he is as much a victim of the craft as anybody else. He may at times look as though he has spoken too much, which is what causes his master's speedy departure; here he may also look as though he has grown cynical and feels free to release his considerable tensions by speaking to the pilgrims without shame.

121. *borwe gold* The Canon is accused of wasting time and materials, holding on to a little of the money in order to buy more supplies for the experiments. He is not accused of outright fraud.

125. *yet is it fals* 'it has always failed up to now'. A succinct statement of the dilemma: he knows it is a vain hope but he cannot resist it altogether.

127. *us biforn* 'ahead of us and inviting us on'.

135. *Catoun* Dionysius Cato, the fourth-century moralist and author of *Disticha de Moribus ad Filium*.

138. *al his sawe* 'everything he said'. The Canon has an inkling of what is to happen now and he may fear that crimes worse than incompetent experimental technique will be revealed.

141. *deere abye* 'pay dearly for'.

144. The Host eggs the Yeoman on and may even be encouraging him to reveal more than he originally intended.

148. *privetee* At this point the relations between the two men become evident quite quickly. In many ways the revelations resemble those that Chaucer makes about each character in the *General Prologue*. A good deal of necessary background has now been sketched and it is possible to advance the relationship.

Notes

149. *fledde* Though this forms the natural ending of the introduction of the prologue, none of the early MSS makes a division at this point.

150. The narrative resumes. The audience is presumably ready for some amusing revelations.

    game a metaphor from hunting.

152. *foule feend* Left alone, the narrator is carried away by his emotions. He repeats himself and uses a large number of devil-images. Words of this type appear more often in this tale than in any of the others.

157. *it is ernest to me* 'it is deadly serious to me'.

161. *I koude never leve it* 'I could never leave it': the chance of success acts as a drug and leads him on.

167. At this point the early MSS start on the tale proper, though there is no need for any such division. In the present edition, therefore, the divisions have been revised.

168. *am I never the neer* 'I can never catch up with it'.

171. *Ther I was wont* 'where I used'.

173. *an hose* A long loose head-covering. This was probably not the fashionable liripipe hat that fell down the back but simply an old stocking which would pass muster as headgear.

174. *colour* The subject of his physical decline is raised again. *Fressh* and *reed* suggest that he was once a golden hopeful youth; now he is leaden in hue. The metallic transformation is, of course, in the wrong direction.

176. *whoso it useth* 'whoever takes it (science) up'.

178. *which avantage* 'that is what is to be gained from the transmutation of metals?'

179. *slidinge science* John Speirs (in *Chaucer the Maker*) draws attention to this phrase as an example of what he calls the 'serpentine deceptiveness' of alchemy. He sees the recurrence of this type of image as the most noteworthy aspect of the entire poem.

180. *I have no good* 'all my goods are exhausted'.

183. *shall it quite nevere* He confesses that he is liable to imprisonment for debt and that he too will have to keep wandering and moving unless he is successful with an experiment.

185. *casteth him therto* 'devotes himself to these paths'.

186. *his thrift ydo* 'all his financial caution and solvency exhausted'.

195. *lerned of* 'told by'.

Notes

196. *no charge* 'no matter'.
197. *there as we shul* 'wherever we mean to'.
198. *elvisshe craft* In this phrase there can be no doubt of the pejorative meaning of *craft*.

     wonder wise 'marvellously learned'.
201. *what sholde I?* 'why should I tell?' The technical terms that ensue are exact scientific language, but their purpose is to create a sense of confusion in the listener who has no chance to slow down the pace at which they fly past him. In this way the sense of bewilderment in the experimenter is conveyed to the reader of the poem: although the alchemist, unlike the Yeoman, knows the meaning of the different nouns, for instance, he doesn't know exactly how they bring about the desired end; while the reader is unsure of the names of the ingredients and the pieces of apparatus.
214. *that of the eyr...nothing* sealed up 'so that nothing shall escape'.
215. *esy fir* The experiments relied a great deal on different levels of heat. Vincent de Beauvais specified as many as nine, which had to be maintained carefully by the use of the bellows. Failure in this particular could easily prejudice the whole operation. *Esy* and *smart* are presumably the two extremes. Ben Jonson makes the same point in *The Alchemist* (act III, scene 2):

> We must now increase
> Our fire to *ignis ardens*, we are past
> *Fimus equinus, balnei, cineris*
> And all those lenter heats.

220. 'In spite of all our skill the experiment comes to nothing.'
223. *a certeyn* The word *quantity* is to be supplied. In this section the polysyllabic rhymes throw emphasis upon the absurdity of the processes and the speaker's lack of understanding of them at the same time.
225. *spirites ascencioun* 'gases given off'. Cf. line 270.
226. *materes* the solids that remain in the containers.
228. With this line it is realized that nothing has come of it all.
229. *twenty devel* The ill-temper of the speaker increases and the number of devils rises at the same time.
234. *lewed* 'ignorant': he makes no pretensions to learning.
237. *boole armoniak* red clay. The correct name would appear to be *bolus armenius*, but it is impossible to decide whether it

is the poet's error to translate it in this way or his way of showing the Yeoman's ignorance.

242. *deere inough a leek* 'costing a good deal too much'.

252. *albificacioun* This process is the projection of the white elixir which was intended to turn metals to silver. *Citrinacioun* (line 263) was to project yellow elixir to turn metals to gold.

253. *gleyre of an ey* 'white of egg'.

254. *donge, pisse* animal excrement was employed as a form of natural heating in experiments of this type but the inclusion of these words acts as a violent form of anti-climax. Jonson, with a more obvious delight in this topic could not resist the opportunity:

> With all your broths, your menstrues and materials,
> Of piss and egg-shells, women's terms, man's blood,
> Hair o' the head, burnt clouts, chalk, merds, and clay.
> > *(The Alchemist*, act II, scene I)

269. *quiksilver* Mercury is 'quick' because it is alive and in a liquid state although it is a metal.

273–8. For information on the astrological element which is blended with the alchemy see *Introduction to Chaucer*.

281. The speaker admits that it is folly to join in the pursuit of 'multiplicacioun' but he is addicted to it. Here he is being direct in his confession.

284. *philosophre* (1) wise man; (2) alchemist. Chaucer uses the same pun in the *General Prologue* of the Clerk of Oxenford:

> But al be that he was a philosophre,
> Yet hadde he but litel in cofre...

Cf. also line 569.

285. *craft so light to leere* 'so easy to learn'. Cf. Chaucer's own statement about the difficult art of poetry: 'The lif so short, the craft so long to lerne' (*The Parliament of Fowls*, line I).

286. *al be he* 'although he is'.

293. *konne he letterure* 'whether he is a bookish person or not'.

294. *As in effect* 'in actual effect'.

296. *multiplicacioun* At this date the word probably conveyed the meaning of usury which was also illegal. The reader may decide whether this meaning may be attached to its use in the present tale.

298. *they faillen*... At the end of another pile-up of words the truth comes out: the learned and the unlearned alike have lost all.

299. *rehersaille* 'repetition'. The Yeoman, having forgotten one series of tasks, runs on and on: he is essentially a parrot imitating the chatter of his superiors.

304. *passen any bible* A hint of the darker nature of the science: a passage follows in which spirits are raised.

308. *al looke he never so rowe* 'no matter how roughly he looks'.

309. *A nay lat be* Unfortunately for the Yeoman he cannot 'let it be', there is the perpetual hope that one more experiment may be successful. Everyone has his impossible and impractical aim in life.

    philosophres stoon The 'elixir' which transmuted metals and prolonged human life.

314–15. The word *he* in these lines refers to stone.

321. *I warne yow* There is a greater poignancy in this passage, which is a warning to everybody to control over-acquisitiveness.

    to seken evere 'it never materializes'.

322–3. 'That hope for the future has made men part with all their possessions.' It has been suggested that in *futur temps* Chaucer is using a grammatical term 'future tense' rather than the simple idea of futurity.

324. *wexen sadde* 'grow heavy and sorrowful'.

325. *bitter sweete* This figure displays both the attractiveness and the repulsion in this career of science combined with magic.

326. *nadde (ne hadde)* 'had they'.

327. *a-night* 'at night'.

331–6. A piece of semi-religious fantasy displaying the isolation and wretchedness of the narrator. The image of infection is important.

332. *brimstoon* The brimstone of the laboratory now becomes the brimstone of hellfire: the traditional imagination takes control of this piece of caricature.

338. *this folk they knowe may* 'thus they can recognize such people'.

339–40. Cf. lines 80–6.

344. *bitrayen innocence* *innocence* here has its religious meaning and implies more than the immediate case.

346. *on the fir ydo* 'put on the fire'.

350. In this line *craftily* certainly implies no compliment. Cf. note to line 39.

351-2. 'Although I know he has a great reputation it has not prevented him from incurring a great deal of criticism.'

354. *the pot tobreketh* The violence of the action is caught in a line distinguished for its conciseness and movement. It reminds us once more of the entrance and exit of the Canon earlier on. Its exciting sound recalls such vivid moments as '"Tee hee" quod she, and clapt the window to' in *The Miller's Tale* or 'Lo where he sit the lechour in the tree' in *The Merchant's Tale*. These have the sharp realization and the vivid sound together.

360. The vessels seem to leap about of their own free will. Even a modern researcher can share these feelings and imagine for a moment that matter has a life of its own.

368. 'Everyone grumbles and thinks himself badly done by.'

369. The change of viewpoint beginning in this line is Chaucer's frequent practice when he wants to present, almost cinematically, the sense of a crowd of individuals.

372. *straw* a favourite mild expletive.
    lewed and nice 'simple and foolish'.

376. *so thee'ch* 'as I hope to thrive' or the more modern 'as sure as I am standing here'.

377. *it was long* 'what was the cause'. Cf. line 369 *it was long*, 'it was lengthy'.

380. *I wol be war eftsoone* 'I shall know all about these difficulties in due course'.

385. *on an heep* 'swept into a pile'.

391. *mishapped have as now* 'has gone badly this time'.

393. *us moste putte...aventure* 'We are obliged to sink our money more deeply into risky ventures'.

399. *craft* The word here acquires the connotation of *ship*.
    in another plite 'to a completely different conclusion'.

400. *and but I do* 'if I do not, let me have the blame'.

401. *defaute in somwhat* 'something was lacking' (possibly 'faulty').

409-12. The proverbs suggest that the narrator's own power of fresh thought is exhausted and he has to resort to these short-cuts to convincing argument.

416. *semeth* The illusion of their hopes is stressed yet again. There are also references to Jesus, to proof, to a thief and to

the conflict of wisdom and folly, all of which ironically summarize the findings of the prologue.

418. *By that* 'by the time that'. At this point in the early MSS scribes have placed '*Explicit prima pars*' and '*Et sequitur pars secunda*' ('End of part one' and 'Part two follows'). But since the tale has not begun and the fictitious tale has still to be introduced, these divisions have been rectified in the present edition.

420. *infecte* The imagery of the prologue carries over into the tale. It should be remembered that poetry in Chaucer's time was intended more for reciting aloud than for silent reading, and that a recurrent pattern of images would only make its effect if it was sufficiently marked. Cf. line 336.

426. 'He has no equal in the world for dishonesty'.

427. *winde* The serpentine image returns. Cf. line 179.

431. *But it a feend be* 'unless (the wight) is as devilish as the canon'.

439. *worshipful chanons* It has been suggested that the address implies a large number of canons present, though the narrator could quite easily be glancing only at the Monk, Friar and priests in the company. However, it is the view of one authority that this tale is not a 'Canterbury Tale' proper and that on the evidence of this phrase it was directed at a group of canons, apparently alchemists, at a kind of summer-school.

442. *ordre* 'religious order' ('every order has its villain').

444. *o singuleer* 'one single'.

446. *correcten* A plain statement of the didactic purpose of the tale. It is helpful to compare with this the comments from the Pardoner to the pilgrims in his tale. He explains his motives without realizing the scandal he is causing and the revelation of his failure as a moral teacher. This is an example of Chaucer's tongue-in-cheek protestations.

450. *Judas* It may be remembered that even Judas the betrayer was seeking to improve things and was deluding himself that by having Jesus detained he might advance the Christian cause. The allusion to Judas is more subtle because of the atmosphere of betrayal throughout.

459. *annueleer* This name was given to a priest engaged to sing annual foundation masses for the souls of the dead. In the *General Prologue* Chaucer gave his judgement on such chantry priests whom he saw as evading the responsibility of parish work.

461. *pleasaunt and servisable* There are undertones here of seduction and lust in the house.

469. *upon a day* A variant upon the formula 'once upon a time'. At last, the speaker has come to his point.

471. *a certeyn* Add 'sum'.

473. *a marc* The confidence trick opens. Once the canon has repaid the sum (13*s*. 4*d*.) the lender will trust him, and so be ready for greater exploitation.

483. *no thing anoyeth me* 'it is no inconvenience at all'.

486. *of condicioun* 'to his bargain'.

487. *breke wole his day* 'keep to the date'.

490. *thing yfallen al of newe* 'a quite unheard-of thing'.

491. *trouthe* 'my word'.

496. *yvele apaid* 'badly treated'.

501. *Kithed* 'showed'.

    gentillesse One of Chaucer's most important words. It has many shades of meaning: good-breeding, unselfishness and generosity.

503. *and if* 'if'.

507. *I wol doon a maistrie* 'I will perform a masterly trick'.

509. *Marie,...hertely* 'By our Lady, I beg you to do so with all my heart.'

512-20. 'See how this thief offered his services. It is indeed true as they used to say that such offers of service are distinctly suspicious. It is also a fact that this canon harboured cursed plots in his heart to bring good people to ruin. I shall soon be able to prove that this is true in the case of that most wicked of all people who takes great delight and pleasure in such courses. I pray that we may be safe from such cunning duplicity.'

516. *trecherie* Images of duplicity return.

527. *fox* The fox was a common animal-symbol of cunning and is used as a devil-symbol in *The Nun's Priest's Tale*.

    yshapen hath 'has planned'.

535. In this line the speaker denies that the charlatan was his master, but reasons for rejecting this are discussed on pp. 9-10.

539. Here *he* is ambiguous. If we accept the interpretation that the two canons are one and the same it is probably deliberate. At the end of the sentence the Yeoman admits that his cheeks glow with shame at the thought of the canon: if it is not his own employer there can hardly be any reason for such sensi-

tivity. It must be assumed that the attempt to distinguish between the two canons has failed and that most critics of the tale are wrong.

544. *reedness* The former self-consciousness returns. The state of muddle and daze, which explains some of the repetition in his utterances, is consistent as a way of characterizing the narrator.

550. *that we it hadde anon* 'so that we can have it quickly'.

561. *coles* The provision of fuel was always a large item in the budget of alchemy. Ben Jonson takes up the same point:

SUBTLE.   Have you brought money
          To buy more coals?
ANANIAS. No, surely.
SUBTLE.   No! How so?
ANANIAS. The brethren bid me say unto you, sir,
          Surely, they will not venture any more,
          Till they may see projection.

                                   (*The Alchemist*, act II, scene I)

563. The first experiment is mounted by the Canon with one ounce of quicksilver in the crucible and one hidden ounce of silver inside the scooped-out lump of beechwood-charcoal. The victim, as was expected in the comic tales of the genre *fabliau,* has to assist eagerly in his own undoing.

564. *crosselet* 'a crucible'.

565. *of* 'out of'.

569. *in name of Crist* The canon, though he takes the name of Christ in vain, is shown to be extremely courteous to his brother-priest victim. His dialogue stands out from the passages of narration which express an irascible temperament.

573. *mortifye* This refers to the process where a metal loses its original substance to be reborn in another state.

580. *poudre* A worthless powder masquerading as the Philosopher's Stone of legend (*the Stone*) which could transmute metals and, in the form known as 'the Elixir', immortalize mankind.

595–6. *noot I wherof that it was ymaad* 'I don't know what it consisted of'.

598. *to blinde with* 'with which to blind'.

603. *graunt mercy* 'many thanks' (*grand merci*).

604. *as that* 'as'.

612. *false gin* either 'engine, device' or 'trap': an excellent ambiguity.

617. *wente atwinne* 'departed'.

618. 'He couldn't rest until he had completely stripped him of his money.'

619–20. This impassioned outburst is only intelligible as another clue to the Canon's identity: it would be excessive in any other context.

621–2. *he is heere and there* The spirit of the absconding Canon is evoked again.

632. *Seint Gile* Originally St Aegidius. He was the saint evoked against such diseases as insanity and sterility. His shrine at Arles was one of the popular places for pilgrimage.

633. *swete* The emphasis upon perspiration recalls the opening of the prologue and binds the two parts of the poem still more closely together.

636. *with sory grace* 'wretched man!'

642. A line of extreme banality which characterizes the falsity of the situation.

647. *so evene aboven* 'so exactly above'.

655–6. The *ingot* (mould) is needed to ensure standardization in both weight and shape for the final testing.

670. The chalk *ingot* (mould) is used to hold silver: once it is transferred to the heat the chalk will disappear leaving only the silver that can look as though it came miraculously into the experiment.

672. *teyne of silver* 'silver plate'.
   yvele meet he cheeve 'may he come to a sticky end'.

685–6. Some of the original MSS of the tale lack these two lines. In most other versions of the text they are included as the end of the Canon's speech, which would make them an aside, since the hearer is not apparently aware of them. Removing the inverted commas from them, as has been done in the present edition, makes them part of the Yeoman's narrative. This makes better sense and retains the separate character of the narration. The smooth canon nowhere speaks in this tone, but it is characteristic of the Yeoman, as we have seen several times before. This difficulty has arisen because punctuation in the early MSS is sketchy or non-existent.

686. *shaving of silver* The silver has simply been released from the cavity in the charcoal. The alchemist suggests that the reproductive power of the quicksilver has been responsible.

Notes

697. The second 'assay' starts here. It calls for a hollow stirring-stick with silver hidden in it. Until the heat mounts the silver remains solid, but when it reaches a sufficiently high temperature the wax melts and silver filings are freed. The victim has only been aware of the stick as a means of stirring the mixture.

700. *crafty* The word is ambiguous here again, although on line 694 it is without overtones of cunning.

713. Note here and throughout the insistence upon accuracy.

717. *in his bisynesse* 'was busying himself'.

720. The animus against the first Canon now creeps into the Yeoman's remarks upon the second whom he claims not to have known personally. This makes the identification of the two alchemists extremely plausible as has been argued in the introduction (pp. 9–10). Cf. lines 539–42.

727. *but it a fool be* 'except a fool'.

728. *out yede* 'poured out'.

730. *wol ye bet than wel* 'what would you find more likely?'

736. *body and good* 'his service and his wealth'.

738. *bihinde* 'still to come'.

743. The third experiment is less carefully administered than the others. It requires an ounce of copper filings fashioned to resemble a bar of silver. The victim is made to fetch some of the materials himself and to contribute to his own undoing. As a result of the experiments three excellent silver bars are on show which will pass any test since they came from the pure metal planted there in the first place. The final trick is the disappearance of the canon with the money for the copyright of his experiment.

747. *ministre of my wit* 'servant of my brain'.

748–50. Cf. lines 539–42 and line 720.

754–72. Here at last the silver plate secreted in the Canon's sleeve comes into action.

767. *unwiting this priest* 'the priest not being aware'.

780. *wite if they been oght* 'find out what they are'.

785. There are now three bars of silver: one with which he started and two fashioned during the 'assays'.

785–6. *in assay To fir and hamer* 'tested them with fire and hammer'.

788–96. With this lyrical outburst—it changes subject at *or for to speke of love*—the Yeoman borrows the rhetoric of courtly love to render the priest more ridiculous.

789. *again the day* 'for the coming of the day'.

795. *stonden in grace* 'stand high in favour'. Cf. the Squire in the *General Prologue*.

798. Religious rapture is parodied by the two speakers as they settle down to their parts in the quest for gold.

799. 'If in your eyes I may seem to deserve to know it.'

800. *receite* 'formula'.

808. This might be about £1000 ($3000) in modern currency.

809. *nere* 'were it not for'.

812. *of nobles fette* 'fetched in nobles'.

815. *I kepe han no loos* 'I do not care for fame'.

835. The tale is over; the ensuing moralization is delivered with a new calm. The verse-tempo of the Yeoman yields to the contemplative one of the poet himself, more suitable to the reflective epilogue.

836–7. 'Strife exists between men and money to such an extent that hardly any of it remains.'

840. An ingenious explanation of poverty: gold doesn't like people tampering with it and in revenge it shuns them.

841. *mistily* This adverb sums up the practical man's view of esoteric alchemy. The Yeoman has been preoccupied, as we know, with the menial tasks and has the outsider's view of it, finding no place within his experience for the spiritual interpretations current in writings of the period.

842. *men kan nat come therby* 'men cannot get to grips with it'.

844–5. 'They might as well chatter like jaybirds and place all their reliance and desire in empty words.'

850. *mirthe* A medieval term denoting general composure and disposition, the opposite of 'melancholy' which also comprehends a much wider range of psychological disturbance than is found today.

854. *they that han been brent* The modern proverb: 'The burnt child fears the fire'.

856. *ye that it use* The admonition to give up alchemy in this line seems to be meant to be addressed to a skilled audience and has been seen as a confirmation of the theory mentioned in the note to line 439.

858. *to long a date* The proverbial saying: 'Never is a long time'. The reliance upon proverbs at this moment in the tale is slightly confusing. Towards the end of the prologue the same trick of style was noted, but here it seems that the poet is acting as his own narrator and discarding the Yeoman-mask. Such ignorance does not accord with the citation of

authorities that follows. The Yeoman, whose mind was superficial and resorted to the short-cut of a proverb, cannot be
imagined as a reader of the alchemical manuscript sources
that Chaucer himself might have known quite well. Chaucer
has allowed the narratorship of the poem to fall out of focus.

860. *Bayard* A proverbial horse and an alliterative line. At this
point a passage from *The Second Nun's Tale* provides a useful
contrast and anticipation:

> Ther lakketh no thing to thine outter eyen
> That thou n'art blind, for thing that we seen alle
> That it is stoon, that men may wel espien,
> That ilke stoon a god thow wolt it calle.
> I rede thee, lat thin hand upon it falle,
> And taste it wel, and stoon thou shalt it finde,
> Sin that thou seest nat with thine eyen blinde.

The poet (as the Second Nun) handles the religious overtones
of which the materialistic Yeoman is presumed to be incapable.
It has already been seen that this epilogue to the tale steps out
of dramatic consistency.

863. *to goon bisides* 'step aside from the true path because of an
obstacle'.

867. *brode and stare* 'you keep your eyes open'.

869. *rape and renne* 'seize hold of and fasten on'.

870. *withdraweth the fir* 'reduce the temperature and the
keenness'.

875. *Arnold of the Newe Toun* Arnoldus de Villanova, a
thirteenth-century French alchemist, author of *Rosarium
Philosophorum*. For information on this important writer see
E. J. Holmyard, *Alchemy* (Pelican Books), pp. 119–23. The
following passage is a translation of an extract from Arnoldus
which demonstrates the poet's debt to him: 'The pupil asked
the philosopher why learned men said that mercury did not die
unless his brother was killed with him...The master said that
Hermes was the first to state that the dragon did not die unless
he was killed with his brother. The meaning of this statement
was that they were as the sun and the moon.' From this brief
extract it is possible to see how difficult it is to unravel
esoteric alchemical literature without a great deal of mis-
applied energy.

879. *brother* According to authorities of the period sulphur and
mercury were two brothers.

Notes

881. Hermes Trismegistus, fabled author of many magical books and founder of the Hermetic philosophy, provided the basis for the signs and symbols of mystical alchemy. This was a development of transmutation into the fields of thought in which man himself might be transmuted into the state of perfection. What might look like chemistry to us could for others refer only to spiritual states. Alchemy bears as much relation to chemistry, it might be remembered, as freemasonry does to architecture, once the secret barriers have been broken down. Such writers as Goethe and Jung have been preoccupied with the mystical aspects of the subject and it is only in this way that alchemy can be said to be alive today.

882. The dragon is the symbol of the god Mercury who is said to die or congeal at the stage of fixation in the great work of transmutation.

887. Sol and Luna were also understood as symbols of male and female principles and presented in the art of the period as a king and queen, sometimes on adjoining hills or in caves.

894. The book *Secreta Secretorum*, familiar to all alchemists, was at one time attributed to Aristotle.

895. The anecdote is attributed to Plato and also to a disciple of Solomon. Chaucer's error may be traced to his authority, the Arabian alchemist, Senior (named in line 897) who wrote an important book, *Tabula Chemica*.

901. *Titanos* Titan, the sun.

902. *Magnasia* A metal variously defined as an ore yielding magnesium and as compound of all four elements (earth, air, fire and water). The persistence of this rudimentary analysis of chemical compounds was responsible for the delay in the advance of the science of chemistry and for continued ignorance of the composition of matter.

904. *ignotum per ignocius* 'discovering the unknown through the still more unknown factor'.

910. The conclusion allows us to interpret Chaucer's view of the future of science. Possibly following Vincent de Beauvais, the encyclopedist, whose work he read and used, Chaucer seems to have foreseen the state in which extensive scientific discoveries would be permitted by God to raise the scope of man's intellect and advance his position in the universe.

926. *multiplie* Although the word means 'transmutation' throughout this tale, it now reverts to the simpler human idea of living a long life and producing children.

927. *point* (1) A point in an argument; (2) a full stop.

928. *boote of his bale* 'relief for all his miseries'. The line can also be interpreted ironically: 'Grant every true and just man this relief—if only such men can be found.'

APPENDIX

In several manuscripts of this tale these lines appear as an epilogue and link to the next tale.

> Whan that this yoman his tale ended hadde
> Of this fals Chanon which that was so badde,
> Oure host gan seye trewely and certain,
> 'This preest was bigiled sothly for to sayn,
> He wenynge forto be a philosophre
> Til he right no gold lefte in his cofre.
> And sothly this preest hadde a luder iape,
> This cursed Chanon putte in his hood an ape.
> But al this passe I over as now,
> Sir Doctour of Phisik I pray you
> Tell us a tale of som honest matere.'
> 'It shal be don yif that ye wole it here.'
> Saide this doctoure and his tale began anon,
> 'Now, goode men,' quod he, 'herkneth everychon.'

Do you think this passage is the work of Chaucer?

BOOKS FOR FURTHER READING

There is very little to read on this tale. Three critics may be mentioned as providing assistance:

T. W. Craik, *The Comic Tales of Chaucer*. (Methuen.)

Charles Muscatine, *Chaucer and the French Tradition*. (Univ. of California.)

John Speirs, *Chaucer the Maker*. (Faber.)

For a specialized study of the background literature the following article may be consulted:

Edgar H. Duncan, *The Literature of Alchemy and Chaucer's Canon's Yeoman's Tale*. (*Speculum*, October 1968.)

GLOSSARY

abit (inf. *abiden*) dwells
ablucion washing of a solid in
    water
abyen pay for
again against; again
alambike head of a chemical
    still
algate(s) all the same
alkamistre alchemist
al that although
alum glas crystallized alum
amalgaming creating a mixture
    of quicksilver and other
    metals
and (l. 49) if
anon soon; now
anonright immediately
anoyen trouble; tire
apayen reward
ape dupe
apertenen belong
argoille tartar
array dress
artow? art thou?
ascaunce perhaps
assay attempt, experiment
assayen attempt
ataken overtake, catch
atwinne apart
aventure venture
avisen consider
avowen tell
axe (inf. *axen*) ask
ay for ever
bar (inf. *beren*) bore
baudy dirty
bechen cole beech charcoal
beden offer

Benedicitee (pr. *bencité*) God
    bless you
berme yeast
bet better
beyen buy
biforn in front, ahead
bigilen cheat
biheten promise
bijapen trick
bisye (inf. *busyen*) make busy
bitimes early
blent deceives
bleren hoodwink; dim
blundren become confused
blinnen cease
bole bull
bolle bowl
boras borax
borwen borrow
botme bottom
brat cloak
brennen burn
brid bird
but (l. 54) except
calcening, calcinacioun
    reducing a metal by heating
casten contrive
cementen seal up
cered closed with wax
chaffare trade
chanoun canon
chit (inf. *chiden*) disputes
chiteren chatter
clappen chatter
clepen (p. part. *yclept*) call
    (name)
clergial learned
clerkes clerics; scholars

Glossary

cloos secret
clote-leef burdock-leaf
coagulat clotted
combust burnt
communen converse, communicate
conceite idea, thought
conclude conclude; succeed
condicioun character
contenaunce pretence
corosif caustic
couchen place down flat
coveitise greed
covent monastery
craft skill; cunning
crased cracked
croper hind quarters of a horse
croslet, crosselet crucible
curcubite container in a chemical still
cursednesse wicked behaviour
curteisye courtesy, courtliness
daliaunce light gossip
dar (inf. *dorren*) dare
deere worth
defaute defect
defenden forbid
demen judge
descensories vessels used to collect droplets
desport amusement
devisen explain
discipline form of learning and training
discrecioun knowledge
disese distress; inconvenience
disseveren separate
dissimulinge pretence
donge dung
doten fool
drede fear; (l. 676) doubt

dressen make ready; go
drough (inf. *drawen*) drew
dullen make dizzy, stupefy
echoon each one, everyone
eek also
in effect in reality
eft again
eftsoone soon after
egremoin agrimony
elixer elixir, the alchemist's quarry
ellis else
elvisshe supernatural
emprise enterprise
empten empty away
enbibing moistening
encorporing incorporating
endetted indebted
enluting smearing with clay or cement
enspire inspire
er (*that*) before
ernest serious
esoteric secret
espide (inf. *espien*) spied out
estaat rank
evene evenly
everichon everyone
exciten incite
experience experiment
expert skilled
eyr air
fain willing, glad, anxious
feend devil
felawe companion
feren frighten
ferforth far
fette (inf. *fecchen*) fetched
flekked spotted
fonden endeavour
foom foam
forgoon forgo

Glossary

fors (see *no fors*)
fourneys furnace
fusible capable of undergoing fusion
game jest
gan did (auxiliary verb) l. 3
gin engine
gladen make glad
gleyre white (of an egg)
gonne (inf. *ginnen*) began
good goods
goodlich kindly
goot goat
governaunce conduct
gracelees merciless
grame grief
gris gray
grope test out
hakeney hack
hals throat
halt (inf. *holden*) holds
halwe saint
han have
hap luck
heeng (inf. *hangen*) hung
hem them
henten seize
herknen harken
herne corner
hewe colour
heyne rascal
hien hurry
hir their
hoomly familiar
hoot hot
hy high
ilke same
impresse throng
induracioun hardening
infecten contaminate
ingot mould
iwis (inf. *witen*) certainly

jape trick
jet contrivance
jocunde happy, cheerful
jupartye jeopardy
kan (inf. *connen*) knows, knows how
kin family
kinde (l. 107) nature; (l. 237) class
kindenesse generosity
kithen show
knowleching knowing
konning knowledge; craftiness
laas string
lakken fall short
lampe sheet
lat (inf. *leten*) let, leave
leden leaden
leere (inf. *leren*) learn
leete (inf. *leten*) let, allow
lemaille metal filings
lenen lend
lernen teach
lesen lose
letterure literature, learning
levere (comp.) rather
lewed ignorant
leyen lie; (l. 43) lay
lief dear
listen (past *luste*) like
litarge lead monoxide
lite (adv.) little
longen belong
loo lo
loos praise
lunarie moon-wort, lunary
luste delight
lusty joyful
maad (inf. *maken*) made
maistrie masterpiece
male bag

77

Glossary

malisoun curse
malliable malleable
maner method
matines morning prayers
matires materials
mescheef, meschief mishap
middleward middle
mis amiss
mishappen go wrong
mite worthless object, small coin
mo more
mollificacioun softening
moodre mother
moot must
morwe-tide morning time
mowen have power to
muchel many; (l. 315) much
mullok rubbish heap
multiplien transmute (of elements)
myrie cheerful
nadde (inf. *haven*) had not
nam (inf. *nimen*) took
namoore no more
nas (inf. *been*) was not
nathelees nevertheless
neer (l. 168) nearer
nevenen mention
nice foolish
nil will not
nis (inf. *been*) is not
noble coin worth six shillings and eightpence
no fors no matter
noght not
nolde (inf. *wilnen*) would not
noon none
noot (inf. *witen*) knows not
o one
oght anything
ordeynen prepare

orpiment arsenic trisulphide
outen show
outher either...or
overslope gown, overcoat
owher anywhere
paas walking-pace
parde by god
paritorie wall-plant: pellitory
passen surpass
pees peace
peyne pain, care
peytrel horse-collar
pie magpie
plite condition
pokket bag
pomley dappled
porfurie slab for grinding chemicals
pouren pore
preef proof
preven prove
priked (inf. *prikken*) spurred
privee secret
prollen prowl
prow profit
prudence expert knowledge
quellen kill
queynte odd, curious
quite requite, pay back
quod (inf. *quethen*) said
rammissh ramlike
receite recipe
rede counsel
rehercen, rehersaille repeat, repetition
referren return
rekketh (inf. *recchen*) cares
relente melt
remanant the rest
resalgar arsenic disulphide
rewen regret; (l. 444) do penance for

78

reyn rain
reysen raise
rit (inf. *riden*) rides
rood (inf. *riden*) rode
roote fundamental
romblen rumble; fumble
rowe roughly
rownen, rounen whisper
rubifying turning red or into gold
sadde weary, satiated
sal armoniak sal ammoniac
sal peter saltpetre, nitre
sal preparat prepared salt
sal tartre salt of tartar
sauf except
saugh (inf. *seen*) saw
savacioun salvation
sawe saying
science knowledge in general
sclaundren slander
sechen seek
secree secret
sely innocent, wretched
servisable useful
shoop, yshapen (inf. *shapen*) created
shrewe scoundrel
siker sure
sith since
sithe time
sleen kill
sleighte trick
slit (inf. *sliden*) slide away
sly subtle
smert(e) (l. 159) pain; (l. 318) suffer
sondry various
soothfastness truth
sorwe sorrow
sothe true
sotted foolish

soutiltee subtlety, trick
squames scales
stillatorie chemical still
stinten cease
strawen strew
subliming vaporization of condensation process
sweten (past *swatte*) sweat
swich such
swink work
swithe quickly
swoot sweat
sy (inf. *seen*) saw
tempren moderate
temps time
terven strip
testes vessels for refining metals
teyne thin plate
than then
theen; thee'ch thrive, prosper; as I hope to thrive
tho then
threpen assert
threting threatening
thridde third
throwe time
thurgh through
tobreken break in pieces
togidres together
tokenen denote
totoren (inf. *torenden*) torn in shreds
trowen believe
tweye two
unnethes hardly, scarcely
unslekked unslaked
unthriftily wastefully
unwit stupidity
up-so-doun upside-down
usage habit
uariaunt changeable
verdegrees verdigris

Glossary

verray exact, true
violes phials, vials
voiden send out
war aware, wary
wenden depart, go
wenen suppose
werche, wereke (inf. *werken*) work
wexen grow
whileer recently
wis wise
wise manner
wiste (inf. *witen*) knew
wight man
wite blame
wit knowledge; reason
witen know, learn; (l. 68) impute
wol wil
wood mad

woost (inf. *witen*) know
worship respectability
wort plant
wreken avenge
wrench trick
yclept (inf. *clepen*) called
ydo (inf. *doon*) done, finished
yede (inf. *goon*) walked, went
ye yes (l. 46)
ye eye
yeman yeoman
yeven given
yfet (inf. *fecchen*) fetched
yit yet
yliche, ylik alike
ymaad (inf. *maken*) make
ynow enough
ypiked (inf. *piken*) picked over
yvele evil
ywis (inf. *witen*) certainly